The
Right
Mind

The Right Mind

Making Sense of the Hemispheres

ROBERT ORNSTEIN

Harcourt Brace & Company

New York San Diego London

The Norman Rockwell painting on page 140 is printed by permission of the Norman Rockwell Family Trust Copyright © 1937 the Norman Rockwell Family Trust

Library of Congress Cataloging-in-Publication Data
Ornstein, Robert E. (Robert Evan), 1942–
The right mind: making sense of the hemispheres/Robert Ornstein.—1st ed.
p. cm.
Includes bibliographical references and index.
ISBN 0-15-100324-6
1. Left and right (Psychology) 2. Left and right (Psychology)—History. 3. Laterality. 4. Cerebral hemispheres. I. Title.
BF311.076   1997
153—dc21   97-21659

Text set in Century Old Style
Designed by Kaelin Chappell
Printed in the United States of America
First edition
E D C B A

*For the two people who have meant
the most to my work about the
brain, mind, and spirit:*

IDRIES SHAH, *who provided a
new framework for spiritual ideas
in the twentieth century.*

ROGER SPERRY, *who opened
a door to the mind many of us have
walked through.*

Contents

Acknowledgments

I thank all those who helped organize and categorize the massive research on the two sides of the brain. I can't really thank everybody, but to those people whose research and library efforts greatly extended mine, I should like to give a citation. Carolyn Doreé of Oxford picked gracefully through the Bodlean's stacks, always seeming to come up with the correct reference and article. Lynne Levitan, of the University of California Davis Medical Center, was extremely helpful and generous, taking time out of her medical studies to investigate mental disorders and the brain, when it seemed that we needed to review all that research.

Jerome Burne helped much in the research on the use of

metaphor and jokes. Denise Winn did yeowoman work on schizophrenia and the right hemisphere and language and the right side. Hania Siebenpfeiffer took the time to go through the libraries in Berlin to find and translate an obscure, but very meaningful, article written in the 1930s on paper that is now so fragile that it cannot be photocopied. Penelope Myers's research on the effects of brain damage has been very helpful. Her new book, *Right Hemisphere Damage: Cognitive and Communicative Disorders* (Singular Press), will be a valuable addition to the field.

Of course, in a couple of decades of reading, some works have proven more influential than others for this book. The book gives its due to Sperry and Bogen's pioneering work, but I have benefitted greatly from Joseph Hellige's *Hemispheric Asymmetry,* especially in the references to work relevant to the view presented at the end of the book. John Cutting's *The Right Cerebral Hemisphere and Psychiatric Disorders* also changed my view on this matter, and it is reflected in Chapter 9. The work initiated by Howard Gardner on the role of the right hemisphere in language, continued by Hiram Brownell and others, too, has been most helpful. Gordon Claridge's work on priming and schizotypy similarly has been influential, although the account of this work was finally edited out of the finished book.

A few score people have read this book in manuscript, from psychologists to general readers to people in writing and publishing. I'd like to thank especially Marc Boggs, Evan Neilsen, Brent Danninger, Alan Parker, Charles Swencionis of the Albert Einstein College of Medicine, and the many others who have asked to remain anonymous.

I'd like to thank Shane de Haven for proofing the book, commenting on it, and providing the office environment without which I would have gone mad.

My editor, Jane Isay, has stuck with me, quietly, often saying nothing, and usually not even sighing, as I have gone through one idea after another, until the progression of ideas in history, current research, and a view to the future came clear.

And my wife, Sally Mallam, abided all the chaotic processes, also read and reread the manuscript, and offered unsparing criticism.

A Prefatory Note

This book is organized into, roughly, the past, present, and future. Concerns about the nature of the human mind have, of course, been with us forever, but it is also almost true that the concerns about the two sides of the brain have spanned that much time.

I'm hoping this book will serve as a one-volume read about this subject, so at the beginning I have gone back as far into the past as I can go, and at the end I have gone as far out (in the old sense) as I can manage. In between, I have tried to highlight the most important current work, and to put it into a viable framework.

Of course, this means that the book moves from the solid ground off into more chancy areas, but this is true, too, to the way scientific inquiry works.

The
Right
Mind

Chapter 1

Mastermind or Moron: Samples of a Pandemonium of Ideas

It's been all around us for years; it is a cliché in general advice to managers, bankers, and artists; it's in cartoons. It is in advertisements. United Airlines offers reasons to fly both sides of you coast to coast. The music for one side, and the good value for the other. The Saab automobile company offered their turbo-charged sedan as "a car for both sides of your brain," the rationale presumably being the cheap-to-run side and the exciting high-performance side. This Saab ad could appeal only to those who don't know much about the brain or have never had their own Saab story.

A friend of mine, unable to remember a name, excused this by describing herself as a "right atmosphere" sort of person, and I suppose this isn't as far from it as any other view.

Many popular writers and educators have written that the right hemisphere is the key to expanding human thought, surviving trauma, healing autism, and more. It's going to save us. It's the seat of creativity, of the soul, and even great casserole ideas. The right side, no doubt.

Another view is that the brain is a Jekyll and Hyde twosome: the left is the rational, conscious, and fully human side; and the right is an automaton, contributing zero to thinking or the higher faculties. Some researchers describe this "Hyde side" as a moron, subhuman in intelligence, and even dangerous.

A biographer lays bare that all of Beethoven's difficulties were due to his being a right hemisphere type of guy. The work cites his miserable childhood, that he was unable to express himself in writing, his handwriting was almost completely illegible, and that his spelling was abominable. Beethoven never mastered the elements of arithmetic beyond addition and subtraction. He even had difficulty with simple things like sharpening his pencils and cutting his quills. He was very clumsy, socially awkward, not to mention deaf. The biographer does allow that Ludwig did write music pretty well.

For the last 25 years few topics have raised such interest, speculation, innovative discovery, and, sorry to say, cacophony in the understanding of the human mind as the differences between the two brain hemispheres. One reason for this is obvious. There's a straightforward and very simple appeal to the research. And it is very dramatic. Joseph Bogen, Roger Sperry, and their colleagues began the modern drama by cutting the corpus callosum, the immense network of 300 million connecting nerve fibers between the two hemispheres of the human brain.

More dramatic still was the outcome. The effect of this surgery was to produce individuals who, on testing, were not able to say what was going on inside their minds. On occasion, one hand would clutch a friend, the other would push her away. Shown a racy image to one side of the brain (through special techniques which we'll discuss later) the person would blush, get all flustered, and then, make up a reason—she would say something like, "That's some machine you've got there," or "I'm feeling very nervous today."

That the brain is double appeals to the conviction that our society has systematically neglected an entire side of human nature. That there are two palpable and distinct hemispheres enables us to identify, correctly or not, this deficiency with a physical side of the brain.

A disclosure: I'm no outsider to the debate. In the early '70s I wrote *The Psychology of Consciousness,* a book that attempted to connect the findings of contemporary psychology research to the conceptions of mind held by religions and spiritual traditions. And I did EEG research from the late '60s to the late '70s, testing which hemisphere was active during different situations.

I didn't continue working on the two sides of the brain since my studies seemed to add a new method to the madness. The controversy raged far beyond anything I had imagined. I went on to other questions regarding human health and the mind and brain, the evolved nature of the human mind and its difficulties comprehending the modern world. I did further work, not about the hemispheres, but a look at the great multiplicity within the mind.

After more than two decades I wanted to take a new look at the enormous amount of research generated on the two hemispheres and two minds. Two surprises bowled me over. First, when I went to do a computer search of the psychological, psychiatric, and biological literature on cerebral asymmetry, I encountered more than 45,000 articles and books that have appeared since I published *The Psychology of Consciousness.*

Second, I began this book with a pretty firm prejudice. I believed that after two decades of research, we'd find many discoveries of more and more differentiation within each of the hemispheres. I wondered whether I and others had unduly credited the two hemispheres with their differences because of the limited research available in the early 1970s.

My assessment then was that two hemispheres would each prove on further research to be a collection of mental modules and that there might be little to distinguish the two sides. And the parade of articles saying that the two hemispheres weren't so different encouraged this view.

Still, as I read and reread, the findings brought me to a surprising conclusion, one that deepened the view of the '70s. The division of the mind is profound, and it begins earlier than we had thought, not in early human society, not in our remote humanoid ancestors, not in monkeys, but before primates. The concerns about the "two minds," too, began earlier and have been a major affair of Western intellectual life much longer than I had thought while writing in the 1970s.

By now it is many years into the enterprise. While the early excitement has flamed off into extravagance, the understanding of the nature of the two halves of the human brain has progressed considerably since I last wrote on the subject, a quarter century ago. I want, now, to present a new concept of how the two sides work, how they evolved and develop in a lifetime.

Its allure has a long history. It was certainly in the air in the '70s to the '90s. William Hollis stated, "The time has now arrived when our posterity must utilize to the utmost every cubic line of brain substance; and this can only be done by a system of education which will enforce an equal prominence to both sides of the brain in all intellectual operations."

To Charles Brown-Séquard the educational system is a failure: "Because of the fault of our fathers and mothers, we make use of only one half of our body for certain acts, and one half of our brain for certain other acts. . . . If children were trained to develop both brain halves, we would have a sturdier and healthier race, both mentally and physically." However, this view was roundly attacked. One critic writes: "It becomes plain that, in the right-handed, intellectual life and progress are by means of the mechanisms of the left cerebral hemisphere. There is no intellect as we understand it except through speech, vocal and written, and the instruments of this function exist only in the left brain of the right-handed, and the right brain of the left-handed."

This was an immense controversy, and it raged throughout the journals, newspapers, and schools. Some had the opinion that the "whole brain" proposals were more like a "whole grain" movement, as they consisted largely of a circle of oddballs and malcontents, they were pseudoscientific and paired with crank beliefs. There was excitement over the role and the importance of the two hemispheres. Education and society had to change. Many of us remember these conflicts all too well.

However, while the arguments cited above took place during the '70s to the '90s all right, they did so in those decades *one century ago*. As these statements indicate, at the end of the nineteenth century there was the same discussion, discord, and dissension concerning the division of the human brain.

And we know that the same controversy raged again in this century. In the *Music Educators' Journal* a professor has it that conventional education has developed the left hemisphere "to the detriment of the 'whole' person" and tends "to minimize and even atrophy right-hemisphere thinking, which is responsible for music processing of stimulus input."

A similar point was made in *Today's Education* by the principal of the University Elementary School of the Graduate School of Education at the University of California in Los Angeles: "The [scientific] findings . . . powerfully suggest that schools have been beaming most of their instruction through a left-brained input (reading and listening) and output (talking and writing) system, thereby handicapping all learners." This principal's views were quoted extensively in the *New York Times* in a 1978 story on "The Brain's Division of Labor."

There were even articles about business management, such as *Harvard Business Review* articles on "Managing on the Right Side of the Brain," or on the left, Right Brain Drawing books, ones on right-brain cooking, photography, and on certain subjects that I cannot bring myself to mention.

And many scientists commented on the research's relevance for society. Roger Sperry, who won the Nobel Prize for his work on the split brain, wrote, the "educational system and modern society generally (with its very heavy emphasis on communication and on early training in the three R's) discriminates against one whole half of the brain. I refer, of course, to the nonverbal, nonmathematical minor hemisphere, which, we find, has its own perceptual, mechanical, and spatial mode of apprehension and reasoning. In our present school system, the attention given to the minor hemisphere of the brain is minimal compared with the training lavished on the left, or major, hemisphere."

Yet Michael Gazzaniga, one of Professor Sperry's associates in the early studies splitting the human brain and who has continued the work, has a startlingly different opinion. He has written that "it could well be argued that the cognitive skills of a normal disconnected right hemisphere without language are vastly inferior to the cognitive skills of a chimpanzee." He offered anecdotes that the right hemisphere was the more impulsive and violent of the two brain halves. He tells the story of the patient who once "grabbed his wife with his left hand and shook her violently, while with the right hand trying to come to his wife's aid in bringing the left belligerent hand under control."

And Gazzaniga's not alone. The neurophysiologist John Eccles thinks that the right hemisphere isn't conscious because split-brain patients cannot express the contents of their right hemispheres in words. He concludes that consciousness resides only in the left hemisphere: "The goings-on in the minor [right] hemisphere, which we may refer to as the computer, never come into the conscious experience of the subject."

The interpretation of the two sides of the brain has led to a mastermind versus moron disagreement in understanding the nature of the two hemispheres. It seems that the question has become an either-or one. Is the right hemisphere just an appendage, speechless, without consciousness, or even menacing? Or is it a mastermind, the locus of higher understanding, creativity, and more?

I believe a new interpretation of the role of the two hemispheres can help to end the dissension, and I hope to contribute to the discussion here. The recent studies of the functions of the two sides reveal the nature of the division of mental processing. In this book I will present some of that surprising evidence developed since the 1970s.

For instance, a man with stroke damage to his right hemisphere looks at a painting by Norman Rockwell (page 140) and describes it: "There are two brothers and a man. They appear to be looking at television. The man apparently is smoking because the ashtray is full of cigarette butts." Others in the same condition also can't seem to "see" what's going on.

Another study, which I'll only mention here as a tease, finds someone we'll call "Wistar" in a darkened room. Suddenly one light flashes, then another, at different intervals, and Wistar tries to guess which sequence is going to follow. Right-hemisphere damage to him and his relatives doesn't affect his ability to predict the pattern, but left-hemisphere damage does. A relative sits and looks at two, three, or four flashes simultaneously, and similarly tries to associate the simultaneous flashes with a reward, and this time right-hemisphere damage affects the thinking. But Wistar and his relatives are not the usual suspects. We'll come to that next chapter.

In this book I will first take a look at the history of the division of functions, one stretching back millennia. Then I will examine how, when, and where the differences in the hemispheres exist and in whom, for much of the current controversy and the attempts at debunking hemisphere differences is based in fallacious ideas about the nature of biological differences. The middle of the book considers the modern research that overturns the original ideas about how the hemispheres operate or, rather, cooperate. I will end with a future-oriented view that the hemispheres differ in how they handle the world, that this difference is ancient, and that it develops in each of us because of events that happen around birth and infancy. This will shed light on the question of the role of the right hemisphere. Is it the source of wit, or is it a half-wit or worse? Does it help us understand our place in the world, or is it a cauldron of primitives? How does the right hemisphere relate to the left? Is it a full partner in the running of the brain, or is it a dullard? Mastermind, moron, or . . .

PART I

Of an Avalanche in the Brain

It is interesting to contemplate a tangled bank, clothed with
many plants of many kinds, with birds singing on the bushes,
with various insects flitting about, and with worms crawling
through the damp earth, and to reflect that these elaborately
constructed forms, so different from each other, and dependent
upon each other in so complex a manner, have all been
produced by laws acting around us. . . .

Thus, from the war of nature, from famine and death,
the most exalted object which we are capable of conceiving,
namely, the production of the higher animals, directly follows.
There is grandeur in this view of life, with its several powers,
having been originally breathed by the creator into a few
forms or into one; and that, whilst this planet has gone cycling
on according to the fixed law of gravity, from so simple a
beginning endless forms most beautiful and most wonderful
have been, and are being evolved.

—Charles Darwin, 1855

Chapter 2

Small Changes, Small Turnings in the Chaotic Evolution of the Double Brain

It is still commonly believed that the human has some completely distinctive characteristics, for example, the possession of language and a high level of artistic and musical abilities. It is my belief that the discovery of dominance *[the specialization of the brain]* in animals will play a major role in removing these last barriers to the special position of humans.

—Norman Geschwind, 1985

Well, it could be a baseball game. They all seem so interested.

—Patient with right-hemisphere damage, responding to a Norman Rockwell painting.*

*The painting appears on page 140.

Each culture seems to have a myth that its people are at the center of the world, and each myth lasted at least until mass communications came on the scene. If we could decode their lingo, we would find that each species most likely believes this too. And our species certainly presumed its superiority.

However, from Copernicus's demonstration that the earth was not the center of the universe to Darwin's investigation that human beings evolved along with other animals, there have been challenges to the idea that humanity is a completely unique species. However, the feeling lingers, and still it's an insult to call a person "an animal." But we *are* animals to the core, for humanity evolved upon the legs, arms, bones, sinews, and neurons of those creatures who developed before we did. Modern biology has made clear that the idea of humanity as qualitatively different from other animals is a conceit.

The thinking persists; for the second half of this century the difference between the two hemispheres has been treated as the unique crown jewel of the human brain. I wrote in *The Psychology of Consciousness* that it was singular to human beings. I was wrong.

The evolution of the different function of the hemispheres is thought to be the moment when we became fully human. It is held to be the time in our ancestor's development when art and literature emerged. Although I'm a great fan of the book *Why Cats Paint,* I would hardly place cat art on the level of Cézanne, or chimp language as approaching that of James Joyce. However, there are divided functions in the two hemispheres of other animals' brains. Very little happens all at once in evolution.*

---

*There is a strong academic and educational tendency to focus on language abilities as the essence of what makes us human. The rational thought developed by the Greeks and advanced for the last two and a half millennia has been considered the unique sign of being human. Of course, no other animals speak as do we, yet there are precursors everywhere of human language, and the hemispheres of many animals seem to be specialized to operate in different ways.

Believing that we are unique may reassure us that we are superior to other living creatures—that we are the chosen species. Yet a closer look reveals our continuity with other creatures. Chimpanzees, monkeys, cats, even rats and mice have a consistent preference for one hand (or paw) over another. And in several birds—including chaffinches, canaries, and sparrows—singing is controlled primarily by the left side of the brain. This quality bears a striking resemblance to the left-hemispheric control of speech in the majority of human beings.

So there are many precursors of the human brain structure. But several moments in the evolution of the brain help to clarify how profound is the depth of asymmetry in nature, and how deep are its roots in ourselves.

These moments are important, because small differences in the past have, over thousands of millennia, developed our ancestors into us. Even individual molecules are left- and right-handed, other animals show preferences for different sides, and brain specialization already exists in the rat. In an important moment in our evolution, humanity had a biological revolution when we first stood on our hind legs, and much later we had a cognitive revolution when we began to write and use an alphabet. Some of these changes are very, very old; some are accidents of our recorded history. Some are as old as the planet, and some are as recent as the era just before Christ (the following chapter chronicles several moments in our intellectual understanding of that history).

First, some ideas that form the background of this book. Many critics of the research on the two sides of the brain have tried to downplay hemisphere differences by proclaiming that the two sides aren't entirely, and aren't always, very different. Some critics note that while spoken language mainly involves the left hemisphere, the right *can* take over speech and writing if the left is damaged. The reverse is true of facial recognition, space perception, and other abilities that usually involve the right hemisphere. And if the damage happens in youth, one hemisphere *can* take over almost all of the functions of the other. Even late in life some language functions of a damaged left hemisphere can be taken over by the right. And not everybody has the right-left difference in exactly the same way, anyway.

These comments are accurate as far as the facts go, but the interpretation is misleading because it confuses our biological potential with our physiology—the way our biology is *used*. I'll explain in the next couple of pages. To do so, I want to propose a different way of looking at the difficulties in understanding the nature of the hemispheres.

Are the hemispheres more similar than they are different? One part of this question is to consider how we make distinctions. Are two people similar to one another? It depends on your standards. They might speak different languages and be of different sexes, builds, and interests. One could say they're completely different, but biologically they're 99.98 percent the same. Is the face of a dog similar to a person's? They have, after all, two eyes, a nose, and the mouth is below the nose and above the chin. The answer, of course, depends on what we compare it to.

Important to understanding the nature of the differences, biological and psychological, is the "winner take all" principle. In American politics nowadays, an election landslide might be a 60/40 outcome. There's a "big winner" here, but there remains a great proportion of the electorate who did not go along. However, even a 51 percent share is a majority and it carries the day, and policies for the entire population change.

This principle, as many politicians know, exaggerates control even when there are small differences. It yields a stable political system, and this means of safeguarding control holds sway, as well, in the brain. Think of it this way: If one part of a conglomeration is more useful, faster, or makes fewer errors doing something, it usually gets chosen to do it.

If you had two stations that could receive the same television program, where Channel 1 receives it perfectly 100 percent of the time and Channel 2, 83 percent of the time, you'd *always* tune in to Channel 1. We use the best of what we have. But if Channel 1's system went down, you'd just switch to Channel 2 with the remote. Similarly for the body: The left and right hands aren't completely different, of course, in writing ability, but a right-hander would never use the left if she didn't have to.

There exists a bodily "winner take all." So, if one hemisphere is "only" 20 percent better than the other at spatial locating, face perception, movement perception, or noun identification, this small difference will give rise to a big difference in how it's used in normal practice. *This* is the difference between biology and physiology. And it happens in everyday life: An accountant who makes 20 percent fewer mistakes or a chef who prepares meals 20 percent more to our taste will be selected much more than their strict mathematical advantage would predict.

And minor advantages add up: Small differences, if they accumulate, can lead to large differences. The process works like compound interest: If the Indians who got that $24 for Manhattan in the seventeenth century had simply put it in the bank at 10 percent interest, it would be *worth more than is Manhattan today*. So that's why investors love compound interest. And with millions of years, changes continue to add up, and that's how many evolutionary changes happen. And they happen within a lifetime, too. One sister who is just a bit better in math may get special training, may qualify for special schools and grow up to be a statistical analyst, while her sister, with only a few percent less innate ability, may not get special training and have trouble balancing her checkbook.

These two ideas, that small differences add up over time to create larger ones and that small differences in potential make considerable difference in use, might help clarify some of the problems in understanding the real differences between the hemispheres.

Here is a classic example of how minute changes can affect a system. In the '60s Edward Lorenz was modeling the weather on a computer. To save time in one calculation, he rounded one of his initial estimators from .506127 to .506. This infinitesimal change gave rise to projected weather results so different in his model that he thought he had substituted one whole continent for another.

Do you know the cliché that a butterfly flapping its left wing just a tiny bit faster somewhere over Japan can affect the storm pattern over Europe? Perhaps that's an inordinate leap, but systems like the weather and the brain are *sensitively dependent* upon tiny changes. Lorenz's "transformation" originated what later became known as *chaos theory*—an understanding of how small changes early on can lead later to very large changes.

Imagine two small boats in a stream—and imagine, too, that first you set one free, then you let the other one go a moment later. You might expect that each would follow the same path, but they never do and may end up on one side or the other of the river. Perhaps one may get stuck on the bank while the other flows along.

Natural forces affect one another ceaselessly. As a result, an infinitesimal change in a system, if early on, be it a small wind turbulence affecting weather, the placement of a pebble in a stream, or trivial alterations in our ancestor's biology, may have unexpectedly large effects downstream.

And by a long series of events—some small, some large, some adaptations to circumstances no longer existing—the two sides of the mammalian brain took slightly different courses. The difference in the sides of the human brain has beginnings in the orientation of molecules and the preferences that our ancestors had for movements to the left or to the right.

The asymmetry in nature didn't originate with the specialized human mind for art and language; it didn't start late in human evolution; it didn't start *in* human evolution; it didn't originate with chimpanzees or New World monkeys. It's pre-*Jurassic,* and so the first evidence is in the fossil record, even in the placement of molecules.

Turning one way or another is important, too. Its origin is ancient and has profound effects on our thought and life. All things turn, and all things also turn in a preferred direction. Pharmaceutical companies now have to be careful that they don't produce a mirror image of a molecule (called *enantiomers*) they wish to sell, for its properties would be different. While all things eventually move in all directions, everything from molecules to mice prefers to orient in one direction or another.

A quirk of nature discovered by Louis Pasteur 150 years ago offers new insights into the unevenness of nature. Pasteur observed that many organic molecules can form in two different shapes, isomers, that are mirror images of one another, just as a right-handed glove is a mirror image of the left. While they are chemically identical, such molecules are physiologically different. Stranger still, living things produce replicas "handed" only one way, while test-tube chemistry as a rule produces an equal mixture of the two. Not grasping this distinction has sometimes led to tragedy.

Consider the orange and the lemon, each with its distinctive fragrance. The smells come from the same chemical, limonene. But the limonene of oranges is the mirror image, the "left-handed" one, of lemons. A reversal in the molecule leads to a distinct smell. The same elements, in the same structure, simply reversed, give off different properties. Lemons turn left into oranges.

Nearly all drugs on the market today are made by synthetic chemistry, and as a rule contain equal mixtures of the two-handed variants. In the past, the assumption was that handed-ness did not matter, but now it is plain that it does. Some chemists believe that the greatest drug disaster of the past 30 years, caused by the sedative thalidomide, might have been averted if the importance of symmetry had been realized soon enough.

The drug, a treatment for morning sickness, had equal left- and right-handed types. But only the *right-handed* portion acted as a sedative, while the left-handed form had highly publicized dire effects: Hundreds of children had been born without limbs.

There are now attempts to produce common drugs in the form of the active-sided molecule, known as a *chiral* molecule, from the Greek for "hand." If it works, in some instances it will be possible to halve the dose of a drug and eliminate certain side effects and perhaps increase the strength of dosages safely.

Life itself is mainly left handed. DNA is invariably so. Other animals have different kinds of distribution of their asymmetry. Flatfish have both of their eyes on the same side of the body; the beak of the New Zealand wry-billed plover is bent to the right to help it turn over stones in the search for food; the fiddler crab has one large and one small claw; in invertebrates the heart is asymmetrical and displaced to the left.

That animals favor different sides has a long pre-Jurassic history. *Elrathia kingii* is not a previously unidentified Abyssinian princess, but the scientific name for a trilobite of the middle Cambrian period about half a billion years ago. *Elrathia* shows a scar that resulted from an attack from the rear by a right-clawed crustacean raider. It's common: Injuries on the right are more than two and a half times more frequent than on the left.

Toads turn, too. In one laboratory study, some ill-fated European toads were required to remove either a plastic balloon wrapped around their heads or a strip of paper stuck to their noses. Sixty percent of the toads used their right paws to remove the balloon and 55 percent to remove the paper strip. This was unexpected, since biologists had thought handedness had evolved in animals that used their hands, feet, or paws to manipulate food or other objects routinely. Toads, it seems, make only limited use of their front legs in everyday life.

Like oranges and lemons, rats turn too. It's thought that their turning is in some part due to an asymmetry of the neurotransmitter dopamine in their brains. With more dopamine production, the rats turn more consistently. Why turn, then, and why would such a reaction persist? Perhaps a consistent turning agenda would help a lost animal return home.

But is it of interest only to the rats themselves or those of us who want to make sure our beloved returns to the sofa at night? No, the same reactions happen in human beings. Stanley Glick, who discovered the rat turnings, also found the dopamine asymmetry in the human brains and did the following: He and coworkers attached a rotation monitor to the belt of his assistants and anybody else they could talk into it around their lab. What did he find happens? There's an unseen human square dance going on! Individuals turn in one direction for the most part. Females rotate more than males and to the left, and males to the right.

And, the ancient propensity to turn has an effect on our daily thinking. Try to answer these questions quickly. How many rooms are there in your house? How do you spell *Mississippi?* In a study in 1972, Katherine Kocel, David Galin,* and I asked people these questions, and found that their eyes turn. They turn away from the questioner when thinking, then in different directions when they reflect on the answer (to the left when counting the rooms in the house, and to the right for spelling).

It took a couple of billions of years, but through a series of steps, from cells through molecules through the first animals and all throughout the time our ancestors stood up and grew an abundant brain and invented written language, it did happen. The brain, beginning as a development of the neural tube, moves on distinct developmental paths with small changes in initial state.

The brain is turned, too. It is not symmetrical, but twisted, as if someone squeegeed it so that the frontal lobes of the right hemisphere rotate a bit counterclockwise. These lobes are larger than the left frontal lobes. However, the rear portion of the left hemisphere, the visual area, is larger than the right. This difference isn't unique to human beings as it appears in the brains of many apes.

There have been many theories of the origin of hemispheric differences. They range from attributing the differences to childhood learning, the way the culture is organized and trains

*At the Langley-Porter Neuropsychiatric Institute in San Francisco.

youth, experiences *in utero,* and the like. Some new research changes the picture.

Remember "Mr." Wistar from the tease in the previous chapter? He was trying to figure out how different simultaneous and successive discriminations work. One of Wistar's cerebral hemispheres was better at discriminating events seen all at once, while the other one was better at figuring out how things happened in sequence. Here's something revolutionary: While the kind of experiment I'll describe could involve an undergraduate sitting in a laboratory or could be a Masai tribesman, a European professor, a six-year-old child, Wistar is the trade name for a breed of white laboratory rat.

If a laboratory rat has similar kinds of specializations in the brain as human beings do, then we have to change our ideas about how fundamental hemispheric asymmetry is. Dividing the world into two ways of organizing must have been useful for all sorts of situations, not just painting and talking. It must have developed long, long ago. The work on the lateralization of this kind of cognitive processing in rats is not better known, partly, I suppose, because it is the product of Russian investigators.*

Most of these experiments took place in the late '70s and the mid '80s. Their basic experiment is very simple: First one hemisphere or the other is inactivated by a drug. (The blood supply goes into each hemisphere independently, and an injection of sodium amitol or similar drug can temporarily suppress the activity of one hemisphere or another, producing a "half-brain animal.")

In this "Wada test" before a brain operation, surgeons inject one hemisphere or the other with sodium amitol and let the person talk to investigate whether it has language ability. It's

---

*Notably V. L. Bianki and E. B. Filippova of the Laboratory of Behavior Physiology of the Institute for Biology, Leningrad State University.

pretty grisly to watch somebody start to talk, then slow down, slur, and stop, and then later to see the right side of their body as it falls limp. However, a few moments later you witness them, much more slowly, begin to come round. But what's interesting for researchers here is that when the same thing (less the talking) is done to rats, their brains and their minds are similarly, if much more simply, affected.

What happened to Wistar is what happens to someone undergoing Wada tests. In the standard experiment, V. L. Bianki and his colleagues gave the Wistar rats a distinction to learn. The rat may have to decide whether one light flashed on before another light or went on after it. Rats typically signal that they've learned this light pattern by pressing a lever to get food. In this test, the left hemisphere in these highly bred white rats was superior to the right in understanding sequence—whether one light came before another, detecting whether one noise came before one another, whether one event in general came before another.

The second study tested how well the rats could judge events that come all at once. The animals were presented with a large dot on the side of one drawing and a small dot on another, or a large dot on the top and a small on the bottom, and the like. And they'd have to tell which of these patterns were similar. Accordingly, a large circle on the left with the small circle on the right matches a large square on the left and a small square on the right. And surprisingly, too, the rats did better with their right hemisphere in evaluating these simultaneous presentations of information.

While most, if not all, emotional reactions are distributed in different parts of the brain, Bianki looked at reactions having to do with the emotional response that a lactating female has to the sounds of her offspring or of other young rats. The strong activation of female rats to the sound of an offspring in distress involved their right hemisphere more than their left. Again, this research provides specific evidence that the specialization of the hemispheres begins a lot earlier in our evolutionary history than we might think.

Bianki also studied the lateralization of concrete and abstract characteristics in the rat brain. The animals were asked to look at geometrical figures that had a size difference of close to two to one. The greater one was always positive—that is, the animal got to eat—the smaller one negative. All the figures were solid, and they were light and against a dark background. Here the question was: If the two figures were presented together, which hemisphere would predominate? And if the two figures were presented in one order or another, which would do better? Again, the left hemisphere did better than the right when the figures were presented in order. That is, neither were there at the same time, and the present figure had to be compared with one in the past. The right hemisphere also did better when both were present at the same moment.

Bianki concluded that "in animals the parallel processor of information processing is localized in the right hemisphere and the sequential processor in the left one. . . . The spatial processor, [and] the parallel one, is located in the right hemisphere and the temporal processor, like the sequential one, in the left."

Perhaps this conclusion is a bit too strong, and I will offer another view later on, but the evidence this group has uncovered leads us to revise the origins of human hemispheric differences. The existence of such different ways to account for the world, this "long ago," that is, when the rat evolved, makes it clear that the division of the human brain into different modes of processing isn't just a matter of upbringing or a trivial fillip on the world, nor is it a division related largely to language versus no-language. These rat studies and other studies like them make clear that there is a fundamental division in animals' contact with the world, and they provide striking evidence on the depth of the division of the hemispheres.

The division is based on a way of approaching the outside world that evolution worked out long before it thought of us. Human beings obviously share many biological components with other animals—the heart, blood circulation, the eyes, and the nose, among thousands. Our divided cortex appeared with the first mammals.

The creationism view is that such structures as the eye could never have evolved by natural selection, for the eye is extremely intricate. The same argument holds for the wing and perhaps language. But in each of these cases there exist earlier adaptations that gave their owners advantages. In the primitive eye, just a basic sensing of light and dark would give an advantage over those that couldn't, and sensing gross movements would help as well.

So each of these ways of organizing reality must have had immediate advantages before there was writing, well before computers were developed, well before modern languages began about 12,000 years ago, well before cave art was painted 30,000 years ago—in fact, well before human beings appeared on the planet. In short, our two sides of the brain are very profoundly different, and this difference runs deep.

Now, evolution doesn't waste its effort, and could not have used the rat as a trial run for us, to set up a system that it knew you would use one day to read this paragraph, annual reports, card catalogs, logic courses, and sewing instructions. There had to be an immediate benefit of the doubled different set of thought processes for animals in any given stage of evolution. And the benefit seems pretty clear.

Having an overall picture would serve very well for an animal getting around in the world. We quickly have to recognize situations that are safe or that have difficulties, and we need to recognize facial expressions, body movements, frame of mind, and other people's or other organisms' intentions toward us.

This ability to assess the immediate situation forms the basis of our social intelligence and helps us judge whether a particular animal is always hostile or friendly. At the same time, rapid and precise actions need a simplicity of attention. An animal can't spend its life forever searching the horizon. A physical reaction needs to be made next, and it has to be one continuous, coordinated movement. The animal needs to make a sequence of precise, rapid-fire decisions, and this decision making seems best done by the left hemisphere. Similarly, in speech, one particular word has to follow the one before; we can't say everything at once. For this an ordered sequencer is most useful, and so there may well have been good advantage in dividing functions long ago in mammalian history. Our recent history, as we'll now see, continues this old story.

Chapter 3

An Avalanche
in the Human Brain

*Boy scouts are sitting there again. I'd say something really
exciting, but this isn't too exciting. I don't know what's happening.
I see a guy sitting there. That's all. And an ashtray there. I don't
know. He shouldn't be smoking around the boy scouts, that's for
sure. If that's where he is. And then there's a little boy sitting at the
end of that bench.*

—Patient with right-hemisphere damage,
responding to a Norman Rockwell painting

Our ancestors had two distinct brain systems in which one
analyzes the world piece by piece, detailing changes, and
the other makes an overall update and applies it until the next
change. This dual function might well have offered a great advantage. First, there would be redundancy in checking conclu-

sions about the nature of events and plans for possible action. Second, two very specialized ways to deal with the world would lead to efficiencies in noticing changes in the world. If a young animal has suddenly become mature and is therefore threatening or now sexually available, another animal needs to know it and change its representation of that member of the tribe.

Do any animals more complex than rats (besides us, of course) have such a system? The answer came from a professor of mine. When I was a graduate student at Stanford University, I worked with Charles Hamilton, assisting him at the lowest possible level in a couple of split-brain operations.

In 1988 Hamilton and his colleague Betty Vermeire tried to answer the question whether, at least, some monkeys have the same kind of specialization as do human beings. They studied a set of *macca mulattas,* New World monkeys on whom they did a fuller brain bisection than did Bianki. (Rats are very difficult to operate on because their brains are so tiny—we called the wire needed to split the brain "mental floss.")

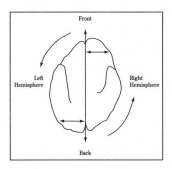

Hamilton cut the corpus callosum, the connecting link between the two sides of the brain, and the other major brain links as well. This produced an animal in which the left eye would then be connected to the left hemisphere, and the right eye to the right hemisphere.

They tested monkeys on a number of activities, but the most interesting result was on facial expression. Expressions provide important information about what an animal is going to do, about whether it wants to fight, to mate, whether it's indifferent, whether it's an animal of one's own species, whether it's harmful or harmless. They found that the hemisphere opposite to the dominant one (the equivalent to the human being's right hemisphere) was superior in picking out and recognizing and analyzing faces.

There's much more evidence: The left hemisphere is larger in monkeys and cats than is their right. Split-brain monkeys were more responsive to videotaped recordings of monkeys, people, animals, and scenery when these were exposed to the right hemisphere than when they were exposed to the left. A similar thing happens in human beings, too.

How did the differences we find in human beings begin? New World monkeys show different amounts of sequential motor control in their hemispheres, long, long before anybody was around to speak or throw. In us, this sequential ability underlies language and logic, but what was it serving in the monkeys? Anthropologist Gordon Gallup describes a "kind of grammar" necessary to swing through the trees. Presumably an animal that remembered better these sequential or "grammatical" movements would survive to produce more offspring.

Human beings possess a system whereby one side of the brain performs step-by-step thinking, which we associate with the highest form of human achievements, and the other makes quick judgments of other animals' expressions and perhaps their intentions. The principle of dividing the brain's information processing into two distinct types seems to be both deep and deep-rooted.

The process of growth and change in evolution is chaotic and filled with conflict. I've mentioned earlier that small changes, early on, can snowball, but sometimes there is a buildup of forces that make small events have wide impact.

When a catastrophe strikes, analysts normally point to a rare set of circumstances or a particular combination of powerful mechanisms. For instance, the 1989 San Francisco earthquake is assumed to have stemmed from very long-term, complex, and slow movements taking place deep within the San Andreas Fault. Similarly, many analysts said that the 1987 Black Monday stock market crash was due to the destabilizing effects of computer trading. And slower events also have their creditors and debtors: The dinosaurs' demise is connected to the impact of meteorites or the eruption of a volcano.

However, systems as large and complicated as the human brain, the earth's crust, the stock market, and the ecosystem can change not only under the force of a mighty blow but also *at the drop of a pin if conditions are right.* Large systems can reach a critical state in which a minor event starts a chain reaction that can lead to a catastrophe or to a new state of being.

Consider a slowly increasing sandpile: First the grains stay close to the position where they land; soon they rest on top of one another, creating a pile that has a gentle slope. From time to time, when the slope becomes too steep somewhere on the pile, some of the grains slide down. This movement can cause a small avalanche. As more sand piles on and the slope steepens, the average size of the avalanches increases; some grains begin to fall off the edge of the circular surface; the pile stops growing when the amount of sand added is balanced, on average, by the amount of sand falling off the edge. At that point, the system has reached a critical state.* When a grain of sand is added to a pile in this critical state, it can start an avalanche of any size, including a catastrophic event. Small changes, at

*The mathematical theory of this process is called self-organized criticality.

the right time, can cause huge repercussions. Think of a match and a forest fire.

In that spirit, here are a set of events that long ago, taken together with the accumulated "compound interest," helped to transform the brain that our ancestors inherited into the modern one.

About four million years ago the forests of East Africa diminished, causing its inhabitants to leave the trees for the ground. Once there, some of them began to stand on their hind limbs. Those standing up saw farther into the distance than their hunched-over counterparts, could carry food in the now freed front limbs, and probably survived better and supported more young. But two things followed our ancestors' standing up: There was increased asymmetry, and a never-equaled explosive growth in the brain.

First, and most obvious, standing up on the hind legs allowed our ancestors to use their forelimbs in a new way. As long as an animal moves on all fours, it needs to be able to move in either direction with any limb, to be equally responsive to a sudden danger or an attack on either side. So almost all animals evolved two-sided symmetry in overall body shape and in their sensory and motor systems. Movements that were too strongly one-sided might produce dangerous responses in an emergency.

But when the first australopithecine or perhaps their immediate ancestors (Ramidus) first stood up, the front limbs no longer directly had anything to do with where the animal is headed. So the human forelimbs became specialized hands and the brain's control of them expanded. The extreme of this is when all the limbs get free of the ground, then cerebral specialization can develop readily. This is why birds' brains are more asymmetric than other animals.

Another help was freeing the forelimbs from the need to support the weight of the torso. Hands could become delicate shapers, not crude supports. In our ancestors all this meant that one limb, usually the right, was then free to become dexterous, a hand capable of finer movements. When this happened, a new era opened up: The brain's original specialization could then greatly increase. Toolmaking and other developments followed and probably served to stimulate further changes to the brain, allowing successive generations to flourish with greater and greater asymmetry.

When our ancestors stood up, the top of the head was exposed to the sun in a degree much greater than any other animal. So the body needed to change, to keep the brain cool. In an amazing adaptation, our ancestors changed in physical appearance and function to shed body heat. They lost hair and perspired more than the great apes. The human intellect was, of course, built upon that which went before, the common mechanisms of sensory and tactile processing, sound processing and two different ways to encode the world. Yet, anyone can see the enormous gap between us and our nearest relatives, the chimps.

Why do we have such a big brain? To speak, to do art and science? Couldn't be so, for, as I said, evolution wasn't going to waste a few million years and a few billion intermediate animals between the tiny ape-like Australopithecus or Ramidus to get, finally, to Einstein or Cézanne. There had to be an advantage to increased brain size before there was agriculture, cave drawings, iron smelting, locomotives, gigabytes of RAM, and twelve-feature movie multiplexes. But this means that at some time, and for a long time, our ancestors had a bigger brain than they could use for thinking.

After the first Australopithecus stood up, there was a period of explosive growth of their brain. It happened approximately at the time of Homo Erectus—two million years ago. The normal explanation is that the explosion occurred as a result of toolmaking, which then selected for bigger and bigger brains to use those tools. Good idea, but the problem with this is that the rise in the brain growth occurred a million years *before* toolmaking, so that theory can't be right.

Something, then, had to spur the pre-human brain on to greater size. That spur might have been packaging requirements given the need to keep the delicate internal brain cells from overheating in the African sun. Note that when you exert yourself, you sweat profusely from the head, not from the muscles you are using. Other animals shed heat through the mouth, as in a dog's panting. The dog, like other animals, has even evolved an elaborate network of blood vessels in the roof of the mouth to aid in heat dissipation. There seems to be a premium in many animals on getting heat out of the head fast.

Consider the brain from the view of packaging its mechanicals. Upright walking put the brain far away from the heart, and more exposed, due to head position, to the sun's heat, although the body overall presents less surface to the sun while standing up.*

The blood supply to the brain changed as well, because it's more difficult to pump blood uphill. At the extreme, the giraffe has a set of valves in its long neck to relay blood. We don't, but we developed a new net of blood vessels that alternatively feed

---

*With a delicate brain one adaptation would be to grow more cells, keeping the inner core cooler. Most of the cells we grow are not neurons but are the supporting cast of cells called the *glia*. These, like packaging material, insulate the neurons, and also allow the neurons to make more connections.

the brain and, when it's hot, reverse the flow to cool it. Some australopithecines had this net of vessels and others didn't. We are descended from those who did. These emissary veins evolved as a radiator, before the great increase in brain size, and probably enabled brain volume to increase.

So the neurons in our brain are more numerous, but more insulated than our forebears'. Because of the extra insulation, we can make connections more easily, like a well-shielded electrical cable. These extra cells and connections, once in place, could then continue the basic plan of asymmetrical development that originated in earlier-evolved animals. There were more cells available, and the brain, freed of having to make the forelimbs similar, could exercise those cells differently.

The small initial differences in the hemispheres continued to increase, and then, and *only then,* during the time of Homo Erectus, did tools and early language further push the evolution of the brain. Language gradually became more and more complex. Then, by 40,000 years or so ago, the brain had evolved enough to enable our ancestors to draw images, to represent concepts. The earliest known organized pictures appear in the caves of Altamira and Lascaux. They are the signs of a fully modern mind. The second system of communication, not in words but in images, had matured.

So there are two systems at the top of the human brain. They govern our abilities to create, in language and in art, and to discover new connections in the world. These two hemispheres appeared in our ancestors as specialized systems sometime during the long period of human evolution. There is evidence for them at least 100,000 years ago and probably earlier. They are, of course, the most distinctively human part of the brain, but built on a long series of adaptations by its predecessors.

After the modern brain developed, toolmaking and the beginnings of society changed the nature of evolution itself. Instead of adapting to the external environment, human society *became* the environment for the most part, and our own evolution was more and more in our own hands. I want to focus on the development of written language, and the modern rise to literacy, which has changed the way our society and our brains work.

How does language affect the brain? In *Language, Thought and Reality,* Benjamin Lee Whorf claimed that the structure of a language determines the reality we perceive. A language with two words for color would lead its users to see the world as bicolored. A culture with few feeling words would perceive emotions plainly, say, as exclusively positive or negative.*

To use Whorf's famous example, the Eskimo may have so many words for snow because they see, and need to distinguish, degrees of slush from dry snow. They have no word, nor do we, for the interval in a restaurant "after your credit card is taken, but has not yet been returned to the table." We know this interval, though, and somebody is probably working on the German longword for it now.

But in the beginning, there were no words, of course. While rats had a laterally specialized and divided cortex, they didn't generate great chat. The modern written language has developed over the past some 40,000 years, long after the human brain first ballooned up and could produce it.

*Whorf's idea made a lot of sense. At one time it seemed to me like the inheritance of acquired characteristics, a beautiful idea that seems obviously true. And like that evolutionary concept, the language-equals-thought theory doesn't work out. If you compare people from cultures with few color words versus those with many, by asking them to match color samples, everybody pretty much acts the same. If you ask people from widely differing cultures to judge emotions, no matter their words, they judge them the same.

The process happened in roughly these steps. Representing things graphically with drawn marks developed a whole new class of symbols, and there is little of this seen before 40,000 years ago. Then there came, perhaps close on to 15,000 years ago, a proliferation of carved and incised "magic wands." These were for the most part engraved bones and carved ivory, found in Spain and Southern France, that contained information on the sun cycle, crops, the movements of animals, and the like. The next step, from 12,000 years ago to about 3,000 years ago, was cuneiform—rudimentary writing developed to deal with trade. Clay tablets were marked with crude symbols that initially indicated what was traded, who owned it, and how many items were traded.

Many of the early codifications of the world started with pictographs—simple representations of an object—and then developed into ideograms, which represented an idea or a word. It is a system that still works for the Chinese and the Japanese today. The phonographic way represents the sound of the language. The earliest ones of this type, which developed from the pictographs and often existed alongside them, would have a picture or letter to represent a syllable of speech, and they are still found today in writing systems such as Indian Sanskrit and Japanese kana.

Numbers developed from simple slashes and were the first visual symbols that had no perceptual relationship to what they represented. By 1800 B.C. cuneiform had become complex and placed a tremendous burden on memory. Can you imagine trying to learn 3,000 different symbols?

To give a current example of the difficulty, even in computers that use little icons to represent a function, it's necessary to put in an overlay (one company calls it "tool tips") that tells the literate user what these symbols mean. We can't keep them all in memory.

This complexity was why the Greek development of the modern and abstract alphabet of about two dozen elements between 1100 and 700 B.C. was such a boon. Instead of having to remember a by-then simplified set of 600 or 700 hieroglyphs or several thousand ideograms, the alphabet needed only 24. It allowed an economical and precise mapping of visual symbols onto spoken language and brought literacy within reach of many more people, even if it was still a small minority. And with the arrival of the alphabet, external storage began to take off.

The most obvious way of representing what someone has said is to draw a picture of it. There are trade-offs: In modern languages you can tell what a word sounds like without knowing what it means, and in pictographs you can tell what it means but not what it sounds like. But to represent the phrase "that rat or bat or cat's hat that sat, down pat, on the mat" you'd need to have a picture of a cat and a picture of a mat and put one on the other. Not to mention the rat, the hat, and the sat. Or the bat and the that. It's not so difficult in English though, since the same element (*at*) repeats.

This simplicity has taken a long time to develop. The most sophisticated Semitic scripts are most similar to our shorthand, a sketch of the spoken word, requiring the reader to supply the context to decipher the text. This makes Hebrew and Aramaic (Arabic matured about a millennium later) and similar languages redolent with resonance, almost poetry in every phrase as the root meanings resound to the listener.

The Phoenician system, and all the immediate descendants of the Palestinian invention such as Hebrew and Arabic, wrote only consonants and the reader worked out what the vowel was by the context, like modern shorthand. If you read "hd n th blk" in a story about someone having their head cut off, your mind would fill in the vowels and read it as "head on the block," while in another context you might read it as "hid in the black."

However, this complexity comes with difficulty. To make sense of a Phoenician or Hebrew text you had to know the context, but in Greek and the following languages like our own, the reading brain could rely simply on the succession of letters without having to check interpretation against what it sounded like. As a result it became possible to read text about new ideas and concepts without having to depend on previous knowledge to decipher them. Most of the knowledge that passed down did so as it had for millennia, through oral tradition and signs.

The intricacy of these Semitic languages, while it may be closer to the truth of describing the linkages and even the fuzziness of our life, is not as precise as are German and English. The reader of Hebrew or Arabic must supply the context between the consonants. So why should languages like Hebrew be read from right to left, while systems with vowels run from left to right?

Almost all pictographic systems favor a vertical layout, while most phonographic systems are horizontal. And out of several hundred phonographic scripts that have vowels, almost all are written toward the right, while out of fifty languages that don't have signs for vowels, all are written to the left. This strongly suggests that there is a good reason for the connection between type of system and direction. And the most likely candidate is that our eyes and brain work in different ways depending on what sorts of scripts they are reading.

Reading toward the right involves movement to the right, controlled by the left hemisphere. And the part of the eye that receives the moving information sends its signals to the left hemisphere. Different orthographies, then, can affect the brain differently. Shape is processed preferentially in the left visual field (using the right hemisphere), while sequence is processed preferentially in the right visual field (using the left hemisphere).

So the Greeks took a few letters that they didn't have a use for because the language didn't use those sounds and made them represent vowels. And then they ended up writing it in the opposite direction, from left to right. It doesn't seem like much, but putting in the vowels actually changed the relationship between the brain and reading.

But what could be the relevance to the brain function of such language phenomena as not having signs for vowels and the direction a text is written in? There are three basic means of reading text, and they are all found both in the past and today. You can go from left to right (as we do), from right to left (as Hebrew and Arabic do), and vertically (as Chinese and Japanese do). Now it could be that different systems use different directions for all sorts of reasons—cultural, habit, etc. But you'd be wrong if you thought that.

It is likely that the culture one encounters at birth and first few years affects the way the hemispheres are organized. Chinese is written up and down, and is largely pictographic and tonal; while Indo-European languages are elemental and sequential, and read from left to right. That's important. By mid-700s B.C., the new Greek alphabet was in use but being written from right to left in the same way as its parent. Within a hundred and fifty years or so it was written in *boustrophedon*—the route an ox plows a field—alternately right to left and left to right. But by about 550 B.C., it had settled down into the familiar left to right, although usually written continuously with no breaks between the words.

A mental revolution happened in the left hemisphere when an alphabetic, full-context language was set, through left-to-right writing. The left side of the brain was already specialized to act sequentially. It was similar to the way the development of the spreadsheet changed the already existing IBM PC. It was an accident, but it made the PC very popular and spurred its development into more and more powerful incarnations. And when it did, it also changed society, at least the business part.

The change in writing became the means of introducing a new state of mind—what historian Ernest Havelock has called "the alphabetic mind." The use of the alphabet converted the Greek spoken tongue into an artifact, thereby separating it from the speaker and making it into a language—that is, an object available for inspection, reflection, and continued analysis. It could be rearranged, reordered, and rethought to produce forms of statement and types of discourse not previously available because they were not easily memorable.

So, does mastering a modern written alphabet affect hemispheric specialization? In modern Greece, Kazos Tzavaras studied the cerebral function of illiterate young men by testing their listening for language stimuli. He used a method called "dichotic listening," which entails presenting different stimuli, such as two different words, to each ear. The person listens to the words coming to only one ear and performs tasks based on that information.

The word "dog" might be transmitted by audiotape to the right ear, and "cat" to the left ear, with the subject instructed to listen to the right ear only, and press a button upon hearing the word for the animal that comes when called. A person with an intact filtering function will press the button when the word "dog" comes to the right ear. If a few moments later, the word "cat" comes to the right ear, with "dog" at the same time in the left, she or he would not press the button, because cats are not known for coming when called.

Literate people use the right ear more for listening to words. This means their left hemispheres are more active. The functionally illiterate Greek men used their left ear and so activated their right hemisphere more than did the literate people studied.

We wonder whether learning a language different from that of the main culture matters. It does, not only because of jobs, *but because I believe that the evidence indicates that learning to read and write a language in youth influences the way the hemispheres work.* This is an echo, but a faint one, of Whorf. The brain seems to develop to a certain extent around the nature of the written language in the culture.

One way of gaining another perspective on the achievements and penalties of the Greek alphabet is to compare it with a completely different system, the pictographic and ideographic systems still used in China and Japan today.

Japanese has both a phonetic script (kana) and a pictographic script (kanji). Research shows that kana is processed better in the left hemisphere, while kanji is handled better by the right. In addition, kanji is more often correctly recognized in the left visual field that connects to the right hemisphere.

And, so, we have a definitive natural experiment: Japanese people who suffer brain lesions in the left temporal area lose their ability to process phonetic kana, both in reading and writing, but can still process logographic kanji; whereas those suffering lesions in the left parietoccipital area suffer impaired processing of kanji but not kana. Reading in kanji still involves a sequential and phonetic process, the province of the left hemisphere, and writing in kanji may also require left hemisphere involvement. So, both kana and kanji processing may be impaired when there is left-hemisphere damage.

There are several intriguing but incomplete reports in the neuropsychological literature that the Chinese don't have a speech-production area exactly the same as we do. And there are other observations that brain damage to Chinese people does not always have the same result as it does to a westerner. It seems that left hemisphere damage doesn't always destroy speech, and damage to the right doesn't destroy spatial and other functions, at least as frequently as the "standard" brain damage to westerners.

We are heirs to the Greek intellectual tradition, one of single-file logic and rational analysis. And it is not only the formal arguments of Aristotle that have been passed down, it is the *alphabet itself,* including its vowel sounds and the way we write it, from left to right, that may play an unexpected role in our brain organization.

So, the development, after millennia of learning to write, of a completely abstract way of representing the world fits in well to the already existing side preference of the brain. It was a glorious accident, but it led to our learning about the world in symbols and, changing the way our brain worked, gave us a way to represent it that could be easily taught.

It's a long tour from those lemons turning left into oranges, to the brain turning left, and those reading the Greek alphabet turning from right to left to left to right and right to left, and then just left to right. Still, this "highlight film," so to speak, makes clear that the basic principles of hemispheric specialization were set in motion long ago, developed long before humanity did, and reached the modern level in ancient Greece. So, it won't be too surprising to find that the first correct explanation of how the hemispheres differ appeared in ancient Greece, soon after the alphabet became widespread.

Chapter 4

Diocles, Marc Dax, Bob Dylan's Hair and Brain, "Tan Tan," and Other Stepping Stones on the History of Brain Differences

By teaching both sides of the brain, society could look forward to a wonderful new world of two-handed, two-brained citizens, with untold benefits for health, intelligence, handicrafts, sport, schoolwork, industry, and the military: . . . If required, one hand shall be writing an original letter, and the other shall be playing the piano . . . with no diminution in the power of concentration.

—John Jackson, 1906

That's probably a young boy—young man. Probably calling on his girl's parents. [cued left]. It's a wooden bench—pine bench.

—Patient with right-hemisphere damage, responding to a Norman Rockwell painting

The divisions of the brain are older than humanity. Yet they are so obvious and so profound that the mental divisions have preoccupied thinkers since the dawn of the modern era, with most of the modern controversies raging throughout our intellectual history. It's surprising how many of the modern ideas have already been presented, some centuries ago.

In the 1970s we chronicled the research work as originating with the split-brain studies of the 1960s. But the nature of the two sides of the brain has puzzled people for millennia. Beginning centuries before Christ and continuing well into the 1800s there was lots of unsupported speculation concerning the hemispheres.

However, an insight emerged centuries before Christ. Diocles of Carystus, in the fourth century B.C., understood that the functions of the two sides of the brain differed, and in the way that most modern scientists see it.* He wrote, "There are two brains in the head, one which gives understanding, and another which provides sense perception. That is to say, the one which is lying on the right side is the one that perceives; with the left one, however, we understand."†

---

*Attribution is often difficult in these cases, for much of the knowledge and the texts themselves of the ancient Greeks went underground, in some cases for a millennium. In this case the conception in question appears in a medieval Latin text found in the second part of a short medical treatise preserved in the "Brussels manuscript" of Theodorus Priscianus, dating from the twelfth century. It, according to those much more in the know about those things than I, reliably quotes Diocles, writing 400 or so years before Christ.

†"An ancient Greek theory of hemispheric specialization" by Gert-Jan Lokhorst (1985) in *Clio Medica,* Vol. 17, no. 1, pp. 33–38. At that time, a few Greeks had already written on this particular division of cognition; Alcmaeon and Empedocles had distinguished between "sensus" and "intellectus," but there is no evidence that their or anybody else's mental distinction was linked with the brain.

While the Greek philosophers and playwrights of 600–400 B.C. expressed many unsurpassed insights into human nature, it's impossible that a complete understanding of the human brain's workings could be this ancient. Brain science was not at all developed then. There was no modern science of anatomy, and the reigning theory had it that the function of the brain was to cool the blood. The brain was considered to be a single mass. The knowledge that the brain is formed of individual components, the smallest ones later called neurons, was to emerge more than two millennia later.*

What happened to this discovery? After Diocles, the idea vanished, probably by virtue of the popularity of accounts of brain function emphasizing the empty spaces, the cerebral ventricles. The insight of Diocles (alas!) then contributed nothing to the later ideas about hemispheric specialization. And others might well have come up with the same idea, but are unknown. But little of that matters, for his insight at the very least shows that philosophers and scientists have been thinking about the question for millennia.

*And maybe his insight was just dumb luck. Diocles' understanding may have been a random shot in the dark in a mottled forest of ideas, and the other random shots might, by now, well have fizzled, with no articles written about them. There exists, as a cliché, a scenario in which one of 100 monkeys, who are seated at typewriters, if not modern word processors, given forever, will type out the complete works of Shakespeare. It is mathematically possible, as anything can happen given enough time.

Still, the odds might narrow with more intelligent scriveners. Given, say, 100 Greeks intoxicated with the new language and speculation, and a few centuries to speculate, one might well find every possible idea, almost, described, the way science fiction writers have probably described everything possible in the next few years. And one idea by chance, might well, or almost certainly will, hit the mark. The idea is harvested, published, and people like me cite it. However, the understanding may well have been random at the time. Perhaps many had the exact opposite idea, or one that held that the left hemisphere was the seat of the flower-planting faculty while the right was the soil.

So, it's thousands of years later when we pick up the story. In 1676 Johann Schmidt described a patient who had right-side paralysis after suffering a stroke and jumbled his spoken words. This was the first unmistakable description of a paraphasic disorder, plus one of the first good descriptions of alexia: "He did not know a single letter nor could he distinguish one from another," Schmidt noted.

The view of the brain that emerged from the classical period was that each part of the brain was duplicated on the other side, as were the eyes and ears. This view was so entrenched throughout the Renaissance that it led René Descartes to elect the single pineal gland as the site where body and mind interact.

Giovanni Maria Lancisi, a papal physician, also looked for the seat of the soul in a single structure. He proposed that it was the corpus callosum, the enormous set of 300 million interconnecting fibers between the cerebral hemispheres, and wrote in 1712: "It is quite clear that the part formed by the weaving together of innumerable nerves is both unique and situated in the middle: and so it can be said it is like a common marketplace of senses, in which the external impressions of the nerves meet. But we must not think of it merely as a storehouse for receiving the movements of the structures: we must locate it in the seat of the soul, which imagines, deliberates, and judges."*

The stirrings of the modern understanding that there might be two different minds in the two hemispheres began late in

---

*In a report to the *Académie des Sciences* in Paris in 1741, the surgeon François Gigot de La Peyronie held that fatal cases always involved the corpus callosum, and that while examining brain-damaged patients before they died, it was evident that the corpus callosum was the seat of the intellect. However, Albrecht von Haller and his students in 1749 severed the corpus callosa of dogs and cats, but the animals stayed alive. Pretty clear proof that the corpus callosum was not, then, absolutely essential to life.

the 1700s. Meinard Simon Du Pui wrote in 1780 that man is *Homo Duplex,* possessing a double brain, and added that "man's nervous system is just as bipartite as the rest of his body, with the result that one half of it may become affected while the other half continues to carry out its proper functions." As the 1800s began, the view grew that the two hemispheres were associated with two minds.

During his early period, Bob Dylan was asked why his hair was so long. He answered that the more hair was growing *out*side his head, the more room there was inside for his brain to grow. A related kind of thinking was the genesis of phrenology, which was to lead eventually to the modern view that many different areas of the brain have different functions.

Franz Joseph Gall's phrenology of the early 1800s originated with the brainstorm that the exceptional word memory of a classmate with large bulging eyes "gave the first impulse to my researches, and was the occasion of all my discoveries." Gall divined that an abundance of underlying brain tissue was pushing this student's eyes, and he determined that the "faculty of attending to and distinguishing words, recollection of words, or verbal memory" resided in the frontal lobes.

Even though Gall had the material to recognize the special status of the left hemisphere for speech, he didn't make the connection. Instead, he believed that each side of the brain could serve as a complete organ of mind: "We have two optic nerves and two nerves of hearing, just as we have two eyes and two ears; and the brain is in like manner double, and all its integrant parts are in pairs. Now, just as when one of the optic nerves, or one of the eyes is destroyed, we continue to see with the other eye; so when one of the hemispheres of the brain, or one of the brains, has become incapable of exercising its functions, the other hemisphere, or the other brain, may continue to perform without obstructing those belonging to itself. In other words, the functions may be disturbed or suspended on one side, and remain perfect on the other."

Unlike the celebrated Gall, who based his wondrous conclusions on a few isolated cases, not to mention the space to be filled by the departure of the bulging eyes, it was the French physician Marc Dax who conducted the first evidence-based analysis of the two hemispheres.

Dr. Dax studied medicine in Montpellier, a beautiful city tucked away in the south of France. He began operating as a military surgeon near the small village of Sommières sometime in 1800. During the Napoleonic Wars, the time of his practice, many individuals came to him with head injuries and cerebral damage.

Perhaps because the findings were so uncommon or because he was, after all, a mere military surgeon working far away from the world centers of knowledge in neurology of Paris and London, Dax waited three decades, like his contemporary Charles Darwin, to write up his observations. In 1836, the year before his death, he wrote a paper that for the first time linked speech directly to the left hemisphere. He presented it at a regional medical congress at Montpellier. Due perhaps to Dax's low status, his own wishes, or the nature of the findings, the paper was published only some thirty years later, in 1865, by his physician-son, Gustav, four years after Paul Broca made his first presentation on the subject—and this began a controversy about the priority of the discovery.

Here's what Marc Dax wrote in his *Lesions of the Left Half of the Brain Coincident with the Forgetting of the Signs of Thought.* Three distinctive patients early on in his practice drew his attention to the role of the human cerebral hemispheres in language function.

> In September, 1800, I made the acquaintance of a former cavalry captain who, having been wounded in the head by a saber blow during a battle, later suffered a major impairment in his memory for words, while his memory for things was preserved in all its integrity. Such a clear-cut distinction between the two forms of memory made me keenly interested in knowing the cause of it. . . .
>
> I . . . inquired of the relatives of the cavalry officer . . . about the part of the cranium which had been wounded. They informed me that it was at the center of the left parietal bone. This reply, which was not at all in accord with the doctrine of the German physiologist [Gall], was, at the moment, useless for the solution of my problem. . . .
>
> From all the preceding [this case, others he cited (see the notes) and his literature review] I believe it possible to conclude not that all diseases of the left hemisphere necessarily impair verbal memory but that, when this form of memory is impaired by disease of the brain, it is necessary to look for the cause of the disorder in the left hemisphere, and to look for it there even if both hemispheres are diseased. . . .
>
> There now remains a very interesting problem to resolve: why does it happen that alterations of the left cerebral hemisphere and not of the right hemisphere are followed by loss of memory for words? While we await a satisfactory answer to this question, I hope that my work will not be useless for the diagnosis and treatment of diseases of this type. . . .

Then in 1861, an M. Leborgne was transferred to Paul Broca, a Parisian neurologist, after a long hospitalization. Leborgne has become known as "Tan" or "Tan Tan" because this sound and a few swear words was all he could speak. This is a common outcome of left-hemisphere damage: I have a friend who lives in Palo Alto who has the same disorder and when he telephones he can only say "on on," but luckily he can now type into a computer that synthesizes speech and can carry on a conversation. "Tan" had suffered from epilepsy since youth, and he had lost the power to speak in 1840 and the ability to use his right arm in 1850. He died six days after arriving at Broca's surgery, and Broca presented his brain with frontal lobe lesions the next day. Four months later Broca gave a full report and presented a strong argument for a localization of the faculty for articulate language in the frontal lobes.

But Broca did not yet realize that language production involves the left hemisphere. The "Tan" case was received enthusiastically and became a landmark that recast conceptions about brain function. Broca went out of his way to show that "his" speech area was different from that proposed by the phrenologists. Because Broca was a highly respected scientist, distinguished physician, founder and secretary of the Anthropological Society, and a Parisian, his ideas were well received.

In 1863, Broca collected more cases of aphasia,* all involving the left hemisphere, and all but one exhibited damage in its third frontal convolution; however, he still had little to say on the role of the left hemisphere in speech. In May 1863, Broca described eight cases of aphasia, all with lesions on the left side.† At the time, this seemed surprising to him. Later that year, Jules Parrot presented the case of a patient who had a le-

---

*Aphasia is simply defined as the loss of language. Carl Wernicke was twenty-six years old when he published *The Aphasic Symptom Complex* in 1874. Like Theodor Meynert—with whom he worked for six months—he believed that all sensory nerves ended in the occipital and temporal lobes and deduced that a lesion of the auditory center in the first temporal convolution left a patient fluent but unable to understand speech or use words properly—i.e., it would abolish sound images.

†In a note in *Bulletins de la Société d'Anthropologie.*

sion of the right frontal lobe without an articulate language disturbance. Broca recognized that this finding also pointed to the special role of the left hemisphere in speech, and in 1864 he described two more patients with traumatic head injuries to the left side—referring to the mounting evidence for left-side involvement in aphasia.

The belief that the left hemisphere is special received a boost in 1874 when Carl Wernicke demonstrated that left-hemisphere injuries were also associated with a more sensory sort of aphasia—a variety in which speech is fluent but not meaningful—named "Wernicke's aphasia." While someone with Broca's aphasia cannot speak words at all, someone with Wernicke's aphasia has speech but it is not informed closely by meaning. A person with Wernicke's aphasia once said to me, "If you could, you could know it, could you, green everywhat, around the bottom, down . . . seeing that, confused, confusing."*

While Broca noted a genuine role for the right side of the human brain in thought, it was an English neurologist, John Hughlings-Jackson, in 1864 who was the first to emphasize its role in understanding the world. He felt that "propositional speech"—our ability to string words in sequential phrases—was perhaps the most conscious activity that human beings possessed. He wrote in 1874: "The right hemisphere is the one for the most automatic use of words, and the left the one

---

*Wernicke also spoke about other types of aphasia, i) motor aphasia—due to damage in Broca's area in the frontal cortex, the supposed seat of movement images, necessary for articulate speech; this kind of patient can understand everything orally and in print, but cannot speak; ii) conduction aphasia—characterized by misapplied words and an inability to read and possibly write, but with fairly good mastery and fluent output; postulated to be due to damage to the pathways connecting the center responsible for acoustic word images and Broca's region. However, Wernicke's most important work in 1874 was based on just ten cases—and of these, only four were backed by autopsy material.

in which automatic use of words merges into voluntary use of words—into speech. . . . The expression I have formerly used is that the left is the 'leading' half for words [speech]." Hughlings-Jackson felt that left hemispheric lesions could "heighten" the activity of the right hemisphere and that comprehension was a function of both sides of the brain. Yet, only the left hemisphere could become "conscious in words."

In 1864, Hughlings-Jackson also raised the point that the right hemisphere may act as Diocles stated, for "perception." And he corroborated it in 1872, when he described a man with a left hemiplegia (a blindness in the left side of the seen world, due to right-hemisphere damage) who could not recognize people, including his wife, places, or things. Hughlings-Jackson presented another such case in 1876, a fifty-nine-year-old Elisa P. who had lost her directional sense; she deteriorated and died three weeks after onset of her illness. Her brain was examined by William Gowers, who found a large tumor in the back of the right temporal lobe. Hughlings-Jackson coined the term "imperception" to describe right-hemispheric lesions leading to the "loss or defect of memory for persons, objects, and places."

Hughlings-Jackson's ideas had much more influence than Diocles', but not all that much, for his concepts were too different from the theories in vogue. They went beyond a simple division between a conscious, superior, intellectual left and an inferior, dark, and mysterious right, giving the right hemisphere a major place in thought.

But Hughlings-Jackson wasn't alone. The turning point for Arthur Ladbroke Wigan's view of the brain hemispheres came while viewing an autopsy. When the dead man's skull was cut open, Wigan was thunderstruck that one of the hemispheres "was entirely gone," even though he had earlier spoken with the man and, as he wrote, the patient "had conversed rationally and even written verses within a few days of his death."

That this man's skull contained only one hemisphere set off this thought in Wigan's complete brain: If a man is able to function well enough in this condition, then was only *one* hemisphere enough to sustain a fully functioning mind? Wigan concluded that if an intact human mind and personality exists in the absence of an entire hemisphere, then we who have two hemispheres must have two minds. The two hemispheres of the brain are two distinct organs, each as well adapted as are the two eyes.

Wigan developed the concept, like Gall's, that every human being was born a double animal, "made up of two complete and perfect halves, and [with] . . . no more central and common machinery . . . than is just sufficient to unite the two into one sentient being." Then the object of education is to concentrate these brains on the same subject at the same time. If they don't coordinate their efforts and remain in synchrony, then a lack of harmony and mental disturbances result.*

Wigan, too, was trying to show that "many of the complicated forms of cerebral unhealth, or mental derangement, are only varieties produced by *the more or less perfect exemption of one of the brains from the disease affecting the other.*" So, he concluded that insanity is present when two brains are in direct opposition. He thought that the hemispheres are not carbon copies of each other even in normal people and that one dominates the other. Madness, he believed, came from a shift in that balance, leaving the two hemispheres on separate courses but struggling against each other, "their separate thoughts jumbling together."

*And he offered up some two dozen detailed and complicated principles and postulates of the actions of the hemispheres.

In opposition to Wigan and Hughlings-Jackson were, so to speak, Jekyll and Hyde. This was the idea that the superior, educated, intellectual left hemisphere had atrophied more than the right in cases of madness and degeneracy. This gave rise, too, to literary allusions to people showing such two opposing personalities, especially the 1880 play *Deacon Brodie: or the Double Life; a Melodrama Founded on the Facts, in Four Acts and Ten Tableaux* by Robert Louis Stevenson and William Ernest Henley. William Brodie, the subject of the play, lived in Edinburgh and was a respected cabinetmaker by day and a burglar by night.

The most famous portrayal was Stevenson's development of this scenario into his 1886 *Strange Case of Dr. Jekyll and Mr. Hyde*. This work makes use of the left hand–right hand duality, the doctor as the portrait of the cultivated left hemisphere and Hyde as the "primitive" right hemisphere that must be restrained.*

By 1869 Broca was writing that cerebral asymmetry was a hallmark of the human brain, and he claimed that the asymmetry was greater in the brains of Caucasians than in other people.[†] It was also "demonstrated scientifically" that female heads and brains were more symmetrical than those of males, and children showed more symmetry than adults. Cesare Lombroso could assert, based on research, that "born" criminals were more likely than upstanding citizens to have symmetrical nervous systems and to be ambidextrous.

---

*I suppose if Dickens had written "A Tale of Two Hemispheres," he might have begun it with "It was the best of minds, it was the worst of minds. . . ."

†This corresponded well with the belief that the brains of white Europeans were notably larger than those of "inferior races." So, Henry Charlton Bastian in 1880 placed "Negroids" between apes and Caucasians on a scale of brain symmetry.

The "research" detected what the researchers believed, and we now know that measurements can be altered subtly when an idea takes hold. Thus, much of the data from Broca's area researchers are incorrect. However, the philosophy of a "barbarian" right hemisphere stimulated magnetic and hypnotic séances that demonstrated that the left side of the brain was virtuous and logical, the right dismal and dumb; in the view of some scientists, the right hemisphere is basically a "chimp."

This prodigal valuation placed on the role of language leading us out of the darkness and the devaluing of the primitive "animal" qualities led quickly to reaction that the "inferior" right hemisphere was not so inferior. It could be educated, perhaps even as much as the "intelligent" left. "Bilateral training" could produce a superior mentality.

Charles Edouard Brown-Séquard believed that the differences between the two hemispheres reflected the failure of school systems to educate the right hemisphere; the left was larger, partly as a function of use. He held that left-hemisphere dominance was a failing in the educational system. Brown-Séquard gave a lecture called "Have we two brains or one? And if we have two brains, why not educate both of them?"*

In it he made the amazing association, one that may link him with Dylan and Gall, that:

> Since the size of our hats grows over the years, this is very strong proof that the brain also grows. . . . In connection with . . . the duality of the brain, there is one point of great importance. . . . It is that we have a great many motor elements in our brain and our spinal cord that we neglect absolutely to educate. Such is the case particularly with the elements that serve for the movements of the left hand. Perhaps fathers and

*Toner Lecture II: 1–21, on April 22, 1874.

mothers will be more ready to develop the natural powers of the left hand of a child, giving it thereby two powerful hands, if they believe, as I do, that the conditions of the brain and spinal cord would improve if all their motor and sensitive elements were fully exercised.

These notions were put into practice and "ambidextrous culture societies" grew to train people to do two things at once, such as playing the piano with one hand while writing a letter with the other. James Liberty Tadd, the director of the Philadelphia Public School of Industrial Art, promoted ambidextral training as part of his effort to introduce comprehensive "real manual training" into the public school system, arguing that parents should train their children to develop both sides of their brain.*

As Tadd explained, "If I work with the right hand, I use the left side of the brain; if I employ the left hand, I use the right side of the brain. . . . I am firmly convinced that the better and firmer the union of each hand with its proper hemisphere of the brain, and the more facility we have of working each together, and also independently, the better the brain and mind and the better the thought, the reason and the imagination will be."

The ambidextralists denounced the folly that wasted half the educational potential of future generations. W. A. Hollis, cited earlier, wanted every cubic bit of the brain used. (Who doesn't?) By the systematic teaching of ambidexterity, Hughlings-Jackson and his followers promised a brave "new world of two-handed, two-brained citizens, with untold benefits for health, intelligence, handicrafts, sport, schoolwork, industry, and the military."

*One of Tadd's major crusades was "The Importance of Contact with Things instead of the Symbols of Things," which is why he emphasized drawing and hand crafts.

This ambidexterity movement was bitterly attacked by the Boston physician George Gould and in England by Sir James Crichton-Browne. Gould had it that "the most foolish, impertinent, ignorant, expensive, resultless and maiming fad is that of the ambidexterity mongers. They do not know what they want, do not know that they cannot succeed, do not know, do not know that they curse the victim of any partial success." In a 1907 lecture, "Dexterity and the Bend Sinister," Crichton-Browne upheld the Broca school that "it is by the superior skill of his right hand that man has gotten himself the victory," and "to try to undo his dextral pre-eminence is simply to fly in the face of evolution."

Crichton-Browne, who had been by this time the British "Lord Chancellor's Visitor in Lunacy" for thirty-two years, was concerned with the supervision of the hospital wards. Perhaps influenced by his profession, he noted that there are periodic outbreaks of ambidexterity and "some of those who promote it are addicted to vegetarianism, hatlessness, or anti-vaccination, and other aberrant forms of belief; but it must be allowed that beyond that it has the support of a large number of highly educated, intelligent and reasonable people, and of some men of light and leading."

So, at the turn of the century, the Jekyll-and-Hyde view prevailed and "whole brainism" was routed to the counterculture. In the 1920s, one such U.S. writer claimed to have brought his two-sided brain

> to such a pitch as to be able to exist on only three hours' sleep out of the twenty-four. Thus from the hour of awakening until 4:30 P.M. he would spend his time in the ordinary right-handed activities of writing, reading, etc. From 4:30 P.M. until 5 P.M. he would perform "left-handed" exercises, at the conclusion of which he would be ready for his left-handed existence. Until

> 3 o'clock in the early morning he would spend his time writing
> mirror fashion with the left hand or reading with the aid of a
> mirror and a table lamp. . . . By thus employing alternately as
> it were the left and right hemispheres, the writer claims to
> have twice the capacity for work of a completely right-handed
> individual.

An early version of the "double your mind power" come-on.

That the right hemisphere was important to normal under-standing of the world withered into the psycho-redemption babble of these proponents. And the flow of ideas went away from the specialization of the brain. Each area of the brain was seen to be equal to all the others, in a debauch of the equal-opportunity ethos of the era.

Thus, the respected researcher Karl Lashley removed pieces of the rat cortex and reported that the more cortex removed, the more learning was hampered. Didn't matter where. Even the discovery that the brain was made up of countless individ-ual neurons didn't matter much. It was an "equal opportunity" brain.

This neurological view synchronized with social movements that emphasized that underprivileged people could develop via enlightened social policies, especially education. If the human brain begins life as an amorphous lump of liquid Jell-O, to be molded entirely by the society, then new wrinkles could arise at any time. John Watson famously claimed that he could take anybody and make him (or even her) into anyone. Later on in this century, B. F. Skinner rode far on this horse to de-velop behaviorism.

For the first six decades of the twentieth century, neurolo-gists and psychologists generally held that the mind was a blank slate. If everyone were born uniform, then universal education and improvements in nutrition could raise the level of civilization. Still, these aims are laudable more for their social good rather than their scientific accuracy. People differ greatly from each other in their biology. There remains the possibility of improving people by their environment; it just would not be the same environmental improvements for everybody.

The stress on equality in the 1930s provided a prepackaged rejoinder to the brutal and fallacious genetic determinism coming out of Germany, Italy, and Japan. It also contradicted the prejudices of people like Broca who were only too happy to prove that females were inferior to males and blacks inferior to whites. Consequently, there was little research on areas of brain specialization, and nothing on the role of the hemispheres. This was in spite of the discovery of deficits due to brain injury.

One contribution during this inexplicable drought deserves mention. It was written in 1936 and is as forgotten as was Diocles so long ago, and Dax for so long. In Berlin, Jürgen Lange studied people whose brains had been partly destroyed by operations, accidents, or inherited diseases. He wrote a chapter in the 1936 *Handbuch der Neurologie* on "Agnosien und Aparaxien," concerning people who had lost their abilities to organize their perception of the world in a logical and useful structure.

These patients lacked the three-dimensional perception that normally distinguishes between the distinct sets of objects in the foreground and the less differentiated images of the background. They completely lost their ability of orientation. Nearly all of them couldn't walk, stand, or name their surroundings anymore because they couldn't distinguish between background and foreground.

Lange then says, in words not heeded, of these patients' loss of the ability to organize themselves in their world, "This fact seems to point out the surprising large importance of the dysfunctioning of the right hemisphere of the human brain. *Somehow the right hemisphere seems to provide the general background of the human worldview.*" [Emphasis added]

PART II

Text and Context:
Our Current Understanding

Chapter 5

The Compass of Laterality

One must remember that practically all of us have a significant number of special learning disabilities.... For example, I am grossly unmusical and cannot carry a tune.... We happen to live in a society in which the child who has trouble learning to read is in difficulty. Yet we have all seen some dyslexic children who draw much better than controls, i.e., who have either superior visual-perception talents, while many of us who function well here might do poorly in a society in which a quite different array of talents were needed to be successful.... As the demands of society change, will we acquire a new group of "minimally brain-damaged"?

—Norman Geschwind, 1972

These two boys are—perhaps their father or their uncle has a bandage around his head—possibly returned from a war. They could be sitting in a church pew.... The boys have very serious thoughts on their mind.... I suppose wondering what their fate might be.

—Patient with right-hemisphere damage,
responding to a Norman Rockwell painting

Flashbulb memories are what we call the tendency to remember what we were doing when horror strikes. This often happens after political assassinations, wars breaking out, the death of a loved one. There was the *Challenger* disaster of a few years ago. Decades earlier, it was the deaths of President John Kennedy, Martin Luther King, and Robert Kennedy, and that marked the minds of my generation. Most of us have never forgotten these moments. I was a sophomore in college when John Kennedy was murdered, and the time of the tragedy was doubly shocking to me. I still recall those drab white halls, and I can see myself walking along slowly as far as the red exit sign to the street. Then I heard the news.

And, more important for this book, I remember what we were learning about in the previous hour. I had just left my physiological psychology class where we were discussing discoveries that I could not believe. I had read that the two cerebral hemispheres of the human brain communicate through the corpus callosum.

My teachers acted as if it had just been discovered. It would have also shocked me then to find out that the corpus callosum had been once thought of as the seat of the soul. It would have been surprising to find that it had been thought important in any way at all. Indeed many physiologists of the 1950s suggested that its function was mechanical, to hasp together the two hemispheres.

OK, you can see that I could hardly credit it when the new investigations were presented in my class, that week, late November of 1963. This is what Drs. Joseph Bogen and Philip Vogel were said to have done: To control severe epilepsy in some patients, Roger Sperry, a physiologist, and Bogen and Vogel, neurosurgeons, decided to cut the corpus callosum entirely.

The theory behind the surgery was that cutting the callo-sum would prevent seizures. In each side of the brain of an epileptic there is a focus of activity. These foci exist at corre-sponding spots, indicating that the brain electrical disturbance responsible for epileptic seizures somehow builds up in one dominant side, then transfers to the other through the corpus callosum. The process cycles, and the electrical activity builds further and further as it swaps around the callosum until the buildup is so great that a seizure results.

Bogen, then, conjectured that cutting the interconnections could prevent this buildup and the seizures might possibly stop. And, as it happened, the patients were generally rid of seizures after the surgery. It seemed daring and outrageous medical care, and it worked, thanks to Bogen's initiative.*

While it is impossible to recapture my astonished reaction to this research, by now, everyone has heard the essential de-tails. I'll be brief, then. I have met some of these split-brain people, patients as well as the investigators, and have even, in a sense, become one. At a lecture, I was once introduced as a split-brained researcher. Confusing the average person with these patients is not as weird as one might think, because the patients appear typical. On first meeting persons who have undergone such a procedure, even after spending an afternoon throwing balls, driving around, cooking some barbecue, watch-ing TV, complaining about the government, they don't appear different from anybody else, save for the flatness of feeling that seems common to severe epileptics. This apathy is due to the

---

*As wonderful as the therapy was, that it was successful in reducing epilep-tic fits has gotten lost in the mental results of the surgery. However, this surgery is not used now due to the success of drugs in containing the outbursts inside the brain.

falls they take and the trauma to their brain over years of seizures, not to the surgery.

At times their mind splits become clear: One split-brain man menaced his wife with his left hand, while the right pushed the attacking hand away. And, shades of Brown-Séquard, these persons have two self-images, as they have two body images, each representing the characteristic approach of each hemisphere. When one split-brain patient was asked about his ambition in life (the answers given separately by pointing with each hand), the right hemisphere (left hand) pointed to a racing driver, the left hemisphere (right hand) to a draftsman. Perhaps the whole person wanted to design racing cars.

It was Arthur Wigan's reverie of two minds severed within one head come to pass. And was the soul, said to reside there by Lancisi, thus split? The surgically separated hemispheres can be tested individually, if the researchers take advantage of the way the nervous system's connections are wired. Roger Sperry and his collaborators found that if patients held an object, such as a pencil, hidden from sight in the right hand, they could describe it verbally. However, if the pencil was in the left hand but out of sight, they could not describe it. This difference in perception happens because the left hand informs the right hemisphere, which has a limited capability for speech. With the corpus callosum severed, the verbal (left) hemisphere is no longer connected to the right hemisphere, which communicates largely with the left hand. In this case, the verbal apparatus literally does not know what is in the left hand.*

*I'm writing this as I experienced it at that time, but to set the record straight, in the early 1960s two reports appeared almost simultaneously that described hemispheric isolation phenomena and clearly attributed behavioral and cognitive functions to the forebrain commissures. These reports were based on two patients: One in Los Angeles underwent a single-staged complete

Sometimes the patients were offered a set of objects out of sight, such as keys, books, pencils, and so on. They were asked to select the offered object with the left hand (connected to the silent right hemisphere). The patients chose correctly, although they still could not say just what object they were choosing. It was as if one person had been asked to do something and another, without knowledge, had to comment on it.

The right half of each eye sends its messages to the left hemisphere of the brain; the left half to the right hemisphere. So, in a demonstration using divided visual input, in which the word "heart" flashed before the patients, with the "he" to the left of the eyes' fixation point and "art" to the right, the split-brain patients responded differently, depending on which hemisphere was controlling the response. When asked to point with the left hand to the word seen, the patients pointed to "he," but with the right hand they pointed to "art."

These findings changed my research interests permanently. However, these reports don't mean much about how the two sides of the brain of an average Joe or Jane differ and how they cooperate in normal life. The sensational differences appear only under the most artificial of conditions, such as putting an object in a split-brain person's hand and shielding it from view.

---

commissurotomy for the relief of intractable epilepsy in February 1962; the other in Boston underwent surgery for removal of a tumor in the left frontal lobe in March 1961.

The postmortem examination in the Boston case in June 1962 revealed marked thinning of at least the anterior callosum. The Boston operation resulted in Geschwind's seminal papers describing the disconnexion syndrome, the phenomenon of behavioral deficits resulting from lesions of cortico-cortical connexions, while the psychological studies of the series of patients who underwent therapeutic commissurotomy following the Los Angeles operation led to a clearer understanding of the specialized cognitive functions and limitations of each hemisphere, and to consideration of the "unity of mind" in relation to neurobiological findings by Sperry and colleagues.

Determining what is affected after surgery is risky business. There is always the uncertainty of making an inference from what's lost in surgery to how things work normally. If we cut off one leg at the knee and observed the person getting around, should we then conclude that the cut-out shin originally contained the stoppage of the hopping reflex?

But how these demonstrations of split mindedness got all our attention! It caused many people to overestimate the split of the mind and underestimate its unity, even though different sectors of the mind handle the world differently. In real life, one disconnected hemisphere isn't operating alone or running the whole show. The two are intimately and thoroughly connected, not only by the corpus callosum, but by all the lower brain structures. And much more.

They are in the same body, after all, even though they're a couple of inches apart. They have the same cerebellum, the same brain stem, the same spinal cord. Each half of the human brain shares years of experiences with the other. They eat the same cereal in the morning and the same burger at lunch (and thus receive the same changes in their blood supply); they share the same hormones. Identical neurotransmitter cocktails mainline through each of them, they listen to the same nonsense from other people, they look at the same TV programs, and they go to the same parties. And neither hemisphere operates anything on its own, any more than we walk with one foot or the other, or whether the area of a rectangle is dependent on its length or width.

There is almost nothing that is regulated solely by the left or right hemisphere. Very simple chores may be the responsibility of one or the other, but both get involved as soon as any situation becomes slightly more complex.

The right hemisphere is strongly immersed in knowing where we are in space, but drawing objects and copying line drawings requires the left. Sufferers of right hemisphere strokes lose musical ability, but in those yet strokeless there is left-hemisphere involvement in musical processes. Similarly, the right hemisphere is the prime mover when looking at simple figures such as dot displays and faces. However, if the person has to tell them apart by one feature, then the left hemisphere dominates.

We do what we do with all we've got.

Do the two sides organize the world differently? Here, some of the more sophisticated split-brain demonstrations provided the first modern evidence that the right hemisphere is involved in the individual's overall worldview. Most right-handed people write and draw with the right hand only. However, almost everybody can write and draw *something* with their left. Joseph Bogen tested the split-brain patients' ability to draw with either hand. Their right hands retained the competency to write but could no longer draw very well. Their left hands could convey the relationship of the parts, even though the line quality was poor.

Now look at the drawings below and try to imagine or copy a cube or a cross with both hands. I'm sure your left hand, if you are a rightie, is simply more wobbly than the right but

produces a similar kind of drawing. Note the right hand of the split-brain patient's performance: The cross contains the correct elements, yet the ability to link the disconnected elements is lacking. Normally, a square would never be considered as a set of disjointed corners! It's as if the parts are simply listed, waiting to be assembled into a framework.

Many split-brain studies confirm that the right hemisphere is superior at assembling the pieces of the world into a coherent picture. Robert Nebes asked split-brain patients to match arcs of circles to completed circles. This requires the knowledge of what the whole circle looks like to be kept in mind. And it's a bit like the test of Bianki's rats' ability to go from the particular to the general. The right hemisphere of the human beings, as were the rats', was superior in doing this.

As startling as they were, the split-brain studies merely opened the door to the important question concerning us unsplit individuals: How do the hemispheres operate when they're *not* separated, and we're doing everyday stuff? After all, most of us haven't had the opportunity to have this operation. This is what concerned me when I began my series of studies on the role of the hemispheres in thought, a series of experiments that took almost a decade to complete. But I've now moved a few years ahead of myself.

After that day in November of 1963, I finished my undergraduate work in New York. After taking some time out to travel, I went to Stanford University as a graduate student in psychology. While I pursued some research work on time experience, I worked on and observed Hamilton's split-brain operations in animals, although I didn't participate in the studies.

After my degree, I went in 1968 to the Langley-Porter Neuropsychiatric Institute in San Francisco to learn about EEGs (electroencephalograms) and their voluntary regulation. The control of brain and muscle processes, with feedback, seemed promising, but its potential petered out over the years. Again, a study of the hemispheres was still in my future.

In the San Francisco laboratory I learned a bit about the nature of EEGs and other brain measures, and found that they weren't an exact or even remotely accurate record of detailed events going on in the brain. They're but a crude indicator of overall brain activity. Because the EEG as well as the later measures like the PET (positron emission tomography) scans remain crude, I'd like to indicate why they're so.

Even though the recording is on the scalp and the squiggles look precise enough to the unaided eye, the procedure is like recording the entire noise from a city twenty-five miles away. If one could hear the city's noise at different times one could find out that more activity was going on downtown during the day, and then spread out into the suburbs at night. What was actually going on, whether deals were made, murders committed, lifelong friendships initiated, soup burned, a new theory of the universe hatched, would be completely unreadable and would, anyway, be obliterated by the rest of the noise. So the EEG, likewise, shows that "something's going on, dunno what" in different areas of the brain.

The brain's workings produce various kinds of electrical waves on the scalp: alpha activity, a synchronous wave, indicates an awake brain on idle, the cells firing in unison; and the faster beta activity indicates an awake brain actively processing information. However, the waves provide no data on what *kind of information* or what the brain is doing.

So, David Galin and I set out in 1969 to select areas of the brain that the split-brain and brain lesion research had shown were involved in different tasks, and to record the brain's electrical activity while a person was doing these tasks. When we did so, we found that ordinary people, doing ordinary activities, turned on and off the two sides of their brain appropriately.

We started by trying the simplest of tests while recording the brain waves. We asked people around the lab to write a letter to someone they knew, and to arrange blocks painted with different colors on different sides. This second test had already been shown to be done better by the left hand of the split-brain patients. (I once saw a run of this study while the right hand was trying to arrange the blocks to match a pattern, got it correct, and then turned the block over. The left hand could hardly be restrained from correcting the mistake!)

We studied Ed Merrin, one of our interns, whom we called Ace. As it turns out, Ace showed beautiful changes in his EEGs. While writing, great alpha waves were flowing over the right hemisphere, signifying idling of that side; and while arranging the blocks, the beta waves, signifying activity, took over the right side.*

A formal test found the same. The right hemisphere showed more alpha activity than the left while writing a letter, and the left hemisphere showed more beta activity. While the person was arranging blocks, the left hemisphere showed more alpha than the right, and the right hemisphere showed beta waves. So when people write, they turn on the left hemisphere and turn off the right side of the brain. While arranging blocks in space, they turn on the right side and turn off the left hemisphere.

We also thought that the acts of reading different material would activate the hemispheres differently. So we compared the EEG measures of brain activity while we had people read

*Ace had been a good test of the model, and it turned out that he became a psychiatrist and went on to write an influential review of the role of the cerebral hemispheres in mental disorder.

technical passages and then folktales. The left hemisphere acted the same with the technical material and the folktales. However, the right hemisphere activated while the subjects read the folk stories, but it did not while they read the technical material.

Technical material is almost exclusively imageless, at least most of the stuff that I read. Stories, on the other hand, generate lots of images; many things happen at once. The sense of a story emerges through style, images, and feelings. So stories can engage the right hemisphere. Later on in the research, and I will return to this later in the book, the involvement of the right hemisphere in language appears much greater than I had thought in the early 1980s.

After Galin and I developed this method it was used in several thousand later studies. The original findings were extended to include emotions, different kinds of thought, the development of the two sides of the brain, and more. And those using similar methods have surprised many of the two-brain enthusiasts. Contrary to popular hopes, all that is good and wonderful isn't all in the right hemisphere. This side of the human brain engages during anger, disgust, and fear, by way of illustration.

It is a puzzle as to what the key is to the combination of applications that seems to reside in each hemisphere. One element is that the two hemispheres seem to be specialized for different emotions, as they are for thought. It was originally believed that the right hemisphere was the seat of emotions and the left, the rational side, would then be the "bad" cold side. The truth, as it has emerged since the 1970s, is more complicated and more interesting.

When people begin to talk, the blood-flow pattern changes in their brains, and there's more activity in the left side than in the right. When they imagine space, the pattern reverses. You may have seen the colored shots of activity deep within the brain revealed by PET scans. These show the metabolic activity inside the brain in almost real time, and the method, while still suffering from some of the limitations of the EEG, is far superior to recording on the scalp. Again, similar though more detailed results have followed.

One can also tap into the hemispheres through the eyes, ears, and different sides of the body. We'll take up the sides later. Although my own work emphasized that one should try to get people to perform things they usually do, in as natural a situation as possible, others had previously used innovative, though artificial, measures to show that normal people do have the potential for hemispheric differences.

Ears first. If you split a sound signal into two, and send it separated a bit in time to the two ears, you can test which ear is better at which kind of material. So, if you play the syllable "ba" to the left ear (which connects to the right hemisphere) and "ga" to the right ear (left hemisphere), what happens? The person says she heard "ga," indicating that the left hemisphere is more activated and competent at this. If you send different musical tones to the two sides and the advantage is reversed, the tone to the right hemisphere will be heard. Melodies are caught better in the left ear as well. Interestingly, this right-hemisphere/left-ear advantage for music changes with trained musicians, as their left hemisphere becomes more active in the listening.

The eyes are divided inside. The left half of each eye sends information to the right hemisphere, the right half to the left hemisphere. To get information into one side or another, an image can be flashed quickly to one half of the eye.* Again, this

*Rather forbiddingly called a tachistoscope (Greek for "measure seeing").

is a highly artificial situation, but one that can yield some confirming evidence. Here, individual letters are recognized better on the right side of the eye (left hemisphere), as are individual words. The left side of the eye (right hemisphere) is better at recognizing dots in different shape and simple shapes. When these are combined, as when a word appears in a fancy typeface, the right hemisphere becomes more involved than when words are in a simple typeface. So, writers, if you want to tickle the right side, put on a fancy face.

Touch asymmetries behave the same. So the brain damage, split-brain, EEG, blood flow, PET scan, dichotic-listening, tachistoscopic presentation, and other measures all agree. This in part is what the 45,000 studies have shown. But later work shows some interesting complexity.

Since the right hemisphere controls the left side of the body and the left hemisphere the right side, are there differences in the expression of emotions on both sides of the body? Leonardo da Vinci's *Mona Lisa* has a smile described as enigmatic, puzzling, ambiguous. Why? Only the left side is smiling, the side controlled by the right hemisphere! Perhaps this is why the expression is so ambiguous.

In an intriguing series of studies, Richard Davidson showed that the left hemisphere may involve different emotions from the right. And the difference isn't that the left hemisphere is grim and the right gloppy and wondrous. The left seems to involve positive emotions such as happiness, and the right negative ones such as anger.

In one innovative study, Davidson gave newborns water followed by a sucrose solution and then by a citric acid solution while taping their facial expressions. They also recorded EEGs from the frontal and parietal scalp regions on the left and right sides. They found the same kind of brain patterns as we did on thinking, consisting of significant activation of the left hemisphere in happy moods, the right in fear, anger, and disgust. This means, surprisingly, that the differences in the hemispheres' emotions, measured by their asymmetries in brain electrical activity, exist at birth. No one, I think, has yet looked to other animals' brains to see if these differences exist, but I'd expect, as with styles of thinking, some precursors at least.

And in the exact same kind of study that we did on thinking, Gary Schwartz and colleagues observed, in frontal zones of each cortex, activation for positive feelings in the left and for negative ones in the right. The same findings occur in the study of brain-damaged adults, too. Another study examined emotional facial expression in brain-damaged adults with right- or left-hemisphere lesions. Patients with right-hemisphere pathology showed less facial emotion than patients with left-hemisphere pathology.

As to why there's such negativity in these parts of the brain, I'd say it's because the right side also manages the large muscle movements (arms and legs) of the body, and the negative emotions require big actions. The internal message from positive feeling is usually "(please) don't stop doing what you're doing" or something like that, while fear and anger may require running, or fighting, or something big in terms of consequence or in terms of the limbs.

Like the existence of such profound asymmetries in animals, the difference in emotion between the hemispheres came to many of us as a surprise, although it shouldn't. Even in the early '70s there were reports of a catastrophic reaction when the left hemisphere was knocked out with drugs (preparatory to surgery) and in cases of massive left-hemisphere damage, and euphoria when the right was unconscious.

More surprising, too, was the research on neglect. This is not the neglect of the right hemisphere in the sense that neu-

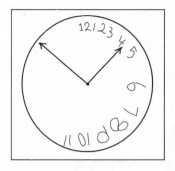

rology and society have done so, but that when one has right-hemisphere damage, typically one can't see or recognize anything in the left side of space. Drawings like this are made by people with brain damage. They neglect half of what's in front of them. One French painter was still able to draw luscious bodies, but somehow they've got no left halves! And some right-hemisphere-damaged patients don't dress well on their left side; men (usually it's men with brain damage even in these days of equality) don't shave on the left, don't brush, etc.

And look at the two houses below (the one pretty dull, the other the same but with a fire coming out of the left window). When right-hemisphere-damaged patients look at these, they say, amazingly, that they're the same, but when asked which might be a nicer place to be, they all say they'd like to live in the one without the fire. If you ask them why, they say, "No idea," or, "I always pick the one on the left." Or "It just looks nicer." I'm sure we'd all agree to take the unburning one!

These findings have been consistent for decades and form part of the lore of left- and right-hemisphere damage. However, after three decades of looking at all of these images, I wondered: How come we almost never see neglect of the right side? Nobody draws a clock face with all the numerals on the left, nobody ignores their right side while dressing, etc.

The answer, I believe, conveys some of the key to the right mind.

It's because damage to this side not only destroys the visual information coming from the left, but more importantly, also destroys the part of the brain that is putting together our understanding of space.

Eduardo Bisiach has offered some extremely interesting demonstrations of this. He asked one of his right-hemisphere-damaged patients, a lawyer, to describe his office as he saw it. The lawyer was able to describe everything on the right, but not on the left. Then he was asked to describe the office, but sitting in front of the desk, not behind it as the lawyer usually did. The patient described the other side of the room perfectly and couldn't imagine the side he had just described! So somewhere in the right side there is a mechanism for putting together the information we receive. When we have left-hemisphere damage, we still can see all of space.

It's commonly thought that systems like the brain and others in the body emerge some way fully formed. In fact they're continuously, if glacially, in modification. The process is like the forming of a large city. My town, Los Altos, began when a banker cajoled the railroad to send a spur in to a point near where he had property. Other businesses built up around it. And later the railroad line was torn down, leaving no trace of any reason for the origins, but the rest remained. This same progression in the brain's evolution makes it clear why there could be no simple way to characterize the hemispheres into, for instance, good things and bad things, as there's no simple way to characterize the difference between Paris and Portland.

Like most cities, the hemispheres weren't designed at all: They developed because of different factors. They certainly did not organize themselves to be understood in a simple academic classification. They're comprised of several different complex systems to handle the body, actions inside the brain, thought and action, and only one of them is the difference many know about, that of styles of thought. But just as cities differ, so the two halves of the brain contain several different kinds of subsystems, linked together by chance, accident, or efficacy.

This isn't a tale of two cities, but of two systems contained in two larger complexes. I'll have more on this at the end of the book on how these two systems grew up around the central early organizing features.

Chapter 6

Whose Hemispheres
Do You Mean?

What resemblance more perfect than that between the hands,
and yet what a striking difference there is!

—Michael Herz, 1909

*There are two brothers and a man. They appear to be looking at
television. More appropriate, I should say, there are two men and
a boy. All three seem seemingly looking at television. The man
apparently is smoking because the ashtray is full of cigarette butts.*

—Patient with right-hemisphere damage,
responding to a Norman Rockwell painting

One oft-made criticism is that the "two kinds of thought
in two hemispheres" concept is exaggerated because not
every brain has the same division of function. However, this is
the case in all biologically based differences. For instance, men

are certainly on average taller than women, but seeing a six-foot, one-inch-tall woman and a five-foot, six-inch-tall man does not make this statement untrue. Biology diverges by degrees; one stomach is larger than another; one nose is longer, another is wider; individual eyes are smaller, more enfolded or exposed; skin color varies in almost all shades; and sharpness of sight or the ability to hear soft tones, to form arguments, or to play the violin differs from person to person.

And there is a big difference in brain organization between right- and left-handers. Scales measure how strongly right sided one is. Some people write, use a paintbrush, kick a ball, throw a ball, or gesture exclusively with their right side, and others may write right-handed but kick left, or throw left, or draw left. The difference in the sides indicates that people have different kinds of hemisphere organization.

So not everybody has the standard differences in the two sides of the brain. A rule of thumb is that about four of five people have the standard division of the hemispheres (this is almost literally true, with the thumb as the exception to the rule and the other four fingers the standard). There are differences between males and females, and right- and left-handers, and in all of it as a matter of degree, some people are highly divided, others more integrated. The differences in brain lateralization are much stronger between left- and right-handers than between men and women.

The left hemisphere is dominant for speech in 90–95 percent of right-handed adults and in 60 percent or so of left-handers. However, there are consistent differences between men and women. Damage to women's right hemisphere generally interferes less with spatial, emotional, and social functions than does comparable damage to men's. The reverse is true for language and such functions: More women with left-hemisphere damage can speak well than can men with similar damage.

Is this sex difference genetic or not? Probably. If so, would one say that males are more specialized and hence advanced or females are more integrated and more advanced? This is a matter of taste. Again, the differences are statistical, and by degrees, and most likely neither speak to advancement. However, these differences are too large to ignore. As individual men and women differ in height or weight, so individual males may have more the type of brain organization seen more often in females and some females may have more the male type, just as some females are stronger than some males.

The most consistent difference between individuals, though, is which hand one uses, and here there are quite clear and consistent brain differences for both sexes. It's obvious that most people are right-handed and some are left-handed. What is not so well known is that a majority of a species' being right sided is unique to humanity. In other species, including the chimpanzees, individual animals favor their left or right side on a fifty-fifty basis. About half of all dogs, cats, mice, and chimps prefer to use their right paw or hand to reach things, half their left. It is only human beings who strongly favor the right hand (90 percent), foot (80 percent), eye (70 percent), and ear (60 percent). Females are slightly more strongly right sided: 90 percent of women are right-handers, while only 86 percent of men are.*

Obviously, built up on the ancient patterns, the change to the left brain/right hand accelerated with the appearance of

---

*It is impossible to say when early human beings or our near ancestors shifted from random handedness to reliance on the right, but it must be at least several million years ago. In one survey of over 1,000 pictures, drawn between 15,000 B.C. and 1950, 93 percent portrayed individuals using their right hand. Microscopic analysis of 200,000-year-old prehistoric tools show 80 percent are more heavily worn on their right side. Further back, there are two-million-year-old skulls of baboons believed to have been clubbed to death by early human beings, the damage indicating use of the right hand.

language in the left hemisphere and with the development of precise toolmaking.

Almost all cultures refer to the left and the right sides, and this comes from observing the nature of human handedness. In the Pythagorean tradition of ancient Greece, the right was associated with the one, the odd numbers, the light, the straight, the good, and the male, while the left corresponded to the many, the even numbers, the dark, the crooked, the evil, and the female.

As Matthew 25:33–34, 41 says, "And He will set the sheep upon His right hand and the goats upon His left. Then Shall the King say to those upon His right, 'Come, ye blessed of my father, and inherit the Kingdom prepared for you from the beginning of the world.' . . . Then shall He also say to those on the left, 'Depart from me, ye accursed, into everlasting fire prepared for the Devil and His angels.' "

Left-handers are a consistent minority, about 10 percent of the population. They face difficulty living in a right-handed world: It is sometimes difficult for them to write alphabetic languages because these were designed for right-handers. Some left-handers write in a hooked position, while others write in the same way as right-handers.

In left-handed people, however, brain organization is often different from that of right-handed people, and there are three types of differences: (1) those similar to right-handers, (2) those whose hemispheric organization is reversed, and (3) those who have language and spatial abilities in both hemispheres. My own EEG studies of left-handers with David Galin and Jeannine Herron show all three patterns of hemisphere organization in different individuals.

And about 90 percent of right-handers are typical in their cerebral organization, while only 66 percent of left-handers are.

Language is spread throughout the two sides of the brain in left-handers. Lefties are more likely to suffer aphasia after damage to either the left or right hemisphere, whereas righties are more likely to suffer aphasia only after damage to the left hemisphere.

An important key to hemisphere differences is that the left is *far more vulnerable than the right.* The statistics on disorder and disease are striking: At least four times as many stroke patients are left-hemisphere ones (paralyzed on their right side), and patients with brain damage are 2½ times more likely to have it on the left side.

The left hemisphere is more at risk even in the womb. The right hemisphere develops first, while the left hemisphere starts late but drives itself harder: Although it normally burns up energy faster than the right, the arteries that supply it with blood bring it less than those on the other side do. So if there is a shortage of oxygen, the left hemisphere suffers first.

This is where the effect of pregnancy and birth stresses on producing left-handers comes in. One of the things that can harm the left hemisphere is the male hormone testosterone. If too much is produced it can slow down development. Then during birth, because of the normal position of the baby's head, the blood supply to the left hemisphere is more likely to be temporarily cut off. Any damage of this sort to the left hemisphere can cause a switch to the right brain and so produce a left-hander. If a left-hander is retarded, schizophrenic, or alcoholic, these problems often are connected with difficulties at the time of birth, such as a cesarean, breech birth, forceps delivery, being born premature, etc.

There's a strong sex difference connected to the hands. Males are much more likely to be affected by complications at birth and are more likely to be left-handed as a result of prolonged labor, breech birth, low birth weight, cesarean delivery, multiple births, or RH incompatibility (mother and baby being of a different blood group). Females are likely to switch to left-handedness if they experience premature birth, prolonged labor, breathing difficulty, or being part of multiple births.

These birth traumas leave some left-handers vulnerable to health problems. They are twice as likely to have sleep problems and be cross-eyed, and 2½ times more likely to be deaf. But most at risk seems to be their immune system, which may be damaged by too much testosterone while in the womb; testosterone, as well as harming the left hemisphere, can also attack the thymus gland, a crucial part of the body's defenses.

Men are not only more likely than women to be lefties but also more susceptible to immune disorders such as allergies, asthma, and hay fever and to autoimmune disturbances. Strong left-handers (those who use the left hand for everything) are 2½ times more likely to suffer one of these than strong right-handers.

Could there have been some benefit to humanity in the presence of a minority of individuals without the usual manifestations of laterality? For some activities, it might have been an advantage to be ambidextrous rather than either right- or left-handed. For example, left-handers may have had the advantage of surprise in early warfare, and may still have it in modern substitutes like boxing or tennis. Judges 20:16 states that, among the 26,000 soldiers of the tribe of Benjamin, "there were 700 chosen men left handed; every one could sling stones at an hair breadth and not miss."

Consider the Kerr family from Scotland, which is 29 percent lefties. Their castles and manor houses have staircases that spiral round to the left so that a left-handed swordsman would have the advantage retreating up the stairs before a right-handed attacker.

Marian Annette, at University of Leicester in England, finds surprisingly that left-handers without birth defects have fewer problems than the strongly right-handed. In her view the right-handedness has been achieved at a reduction in the efficiency of the right hemisphere. Left-handers who don't have a weakened right hemisphere do better at a wide range of tasks, with the exception of the early development of language.

There are undoubtedly left-handers who favor that side because of brain damage at birth, but chances are that most left-handers simply have a different brain organization from right-handers. That may mean some early problems with speech and language, which may well be compensated by superior math ability. In terms of a career, architecture or fencing might be a better bet than linguistic philosophy, but such advice could just as well fit a mild right-hander.

This very brief look at the way right- and left-handers, men and women, use their brains shows that the basic difference in hemispheres is modified in different individuals, just as is the basic face or verbal ability. Not everybody conforms to the typical left and right pattern or the male or female pattern. But some of the deviations show, as with other biological phenomena, that the division of function of the two sides is the main rule.

Chapter 7

The Run of Dichotomania

The historic meeting of Cortés and Montezuma . . . illustrates
an improbable encounter of two disparate personalities and
civilizations, one literate, controlled by rigid left hemispheric
programming and ideologies, the other by what Julian
Jaynes called the bicameral mind, presided over by the right
hemisphere, the sounding board of the hallucinatory voices
of dead kings and immortal gods.   —Jan Ehrenwald, 1984

They're at the movies and they're watching a moving picture.
Probably an action picture.

—Patient with right-hemisphere damage,
responding to a Norman Rockwell painting

O f course, Montezuma did get his revenge on Western culture when the right-hemisphere emancipation movement
of the 1970s erupted into areas such as Beethoven biography,

photography, drawing, cooking, auto repair, and housekeeping. A questionnaire of twenty-one items in the *Chicago Tribune,* by two professors of education at Brigham Young University, invited its readers to "Test yourself: Are you right-brained or left-brained?"

The promoter of whole-brain learning promised brain-mind expansion through the use of megasubliminal tape recordings. Unlike "mere motivation tapes," these are "7 leveled or tracked—3 hearable by left brain and 4 hearable by right brain—bypassing your resistance to positive change." Tapes then cost $195 and were advertised regularly in the *New York Times* during the '80s. There's even a fairly recent book, by a mainline publisher, with the title *Right Brain Sex,* no kidding. I couldn't bring myself to open it.

Sometimes, when asked about all this work, I feel that we are at the moment in *The Godfather* when the old Don Corleone presides at a meeting and asks, "How could things have gotten so out of hand?" How did all these well-motivated people get so far away from the evidence and even the scientific theorizing? It all started with good ideas, good intentions, and good works.

In 1969, Joseph Bogen proposed a classification for the two brain halves that ran counter to the mid-twentieth-century habit of treating the left side of the brain as dominant and the right side as primitive. In Bogen's view, the human "propositional" left hemisphere is complemented by an "appositional mind" on the right side. This "other" brain processes information in a nonlinear, synthetic mode characteristic of musical and artistic expression.

He went on to speculate that the age-old tendency for societies to dichotomize human experience (pitting reason against intuition, science against art, etc.) might reflect that "there are two types of thinking generated in the same cerebrum." He felt it likely that, not just split-brain patients, but all people pass through life with two functionally independent and cognitively complementary brains. He called his perspective neowiganism, in tribute to Wigan's *Duality of Mind*.

Bogen's assessment is that our society has overstressed the three R's in the school system and has educated students lopsidedly toward left-propositional thinking rather than right-appositional thinking. His opinion gave rise to the idea that educators should encourage more right-hemisphere learning in the classroom (i.e., the artistic and musical talents, the creative insights, as well as the spatial problem-solving abilities). He backed the use of different instructional techniques to boost right-hemisphere thinking and new tests: To this end, more hands-on laboratories and field experiences should be included in the educational curriculum, at the expense of more traditional lectures and seminars.

Who are the right-brained individuals? A disproportionately large number have been reported to be members of certain ethnic and racial minorities; some investigators have concluded that Hopi Indians and urban blacks were relatively more right-hemispheric in their thinking than were whites. Other investigations in the late 1970s showed similar results, authors of reports explaining these differences as manifestations of the roles of language and culture.

Sometimes Native Americans, blacks, and other "right-brain dominant" individuals were held up by some of Bogen's followers as models to be admired and emulated by the left-brained majority. This seems acutely careless, somehow confusing a better right hemisphere with a worse verbal and analytical education. There had to be a more appropriate way to look at differences between traditions.

In *The Psychology of Consciousness,* I wrote that we could well understand different thought forms and norms as involving the brain's cerebral hemispheres in differing proportions. Thus, the vows of silence, the stopping of verbal thought, the dancing, the concentration on the body and on spatial images, and the wisdom stories all might be thought of as engaging the right hemisphere while suppressing the left. Later research showed that reading Sufi stories did engage the right hemisphere, and doing tasks nonverbally did suppress the left. And the restraint of speech and stopping of thought are obvious as ways to suppress the left side.

My hope was to open a different way of understanding about what people in different cultures and traditions were doing, so as not to reject them as insufficiently logical and scientific, when they weren't trying to do that at all. I spoke at some conferences, raising these questions to reconsider how we taught the curriculum. Still the movement it seemed to liberate left me far behind. I never expected that this new look at the brain and cognition would take on a life of its own.

Others took Bogen's lead and moved both with and without any scientific backup into cultural concerns, from different biases. So, brain researcher Michael Gazzaniga justifies conservative social policies on the basis of the splits in the brain. In *The Social Brain* (Basic Books, 1985), he writes:

> The left brain is constantly and reflexively generating theories to explain the internal and external events that occur around us. And it is because of that structure that we always attribute causes to everything that happens to us.
>
> Now it turns out that most of us think things are not going our way as often as they should, and we like to find external causes for our dissatisfaction. . . . Needless to say, these processes are also active in people heavily dependent on . . .

> social programs. That is why structuring an artificial, make-do
> environment that elicits dependent behaviors is so dangerous.
> The interpreter module [the important component he believes
> exists in the left hemisphere] is going to have to make sense
> out of such a strange world, and beliefs about the nature of
> things emerging in such an environment are going to become
> quite odd.

Gazzaniga certainly knows a great amount about the brain, but he doesn't understand as much about psychological and political thought. One could easily argue the opposite of his position. But this is the point: Many people have tried to justify their own personal attitudes toward almost any issue—art, politics, business management, education, and here even social programs—on this kind of research. Most of it was by people who were less well-grounded than Gazzinaga in the research but similarly misguided.

Betty Edwards's *Drawing on the Right Side of the Brain* has been wildly popular. It recommends that drawing students rouse their right hemispheres for freer expression. Edwards's exercises consist of copying objects that are presented upside-down, so that the left hemisphere is supposed not to be able to label or analyze the items because they will be unrecognizable. Accordingly, the right hemisphere is supposed to exercise its holistic style fully, without being inhibited by its analytic counterpart. While many of the procedures in this pretty good book are probably great for artists on their own merit, and are similar to the classical techniques, they aren't genuinely based on the brain's workings.

Katheryn Marx got interested by "seeing two photographs of the same place that reflected two completely different approaches to the subject, both of which the artist considered to be equally representative of the location." As she explains, "I recognized that the impulses for the two photographic perspectives came from two different 'places' within the artist." Marx thus distinguishes between two different kinds of photography and photographers:

> Left-brain-oriented pictures are more directed, previsualized, and literal than right-brain-oriented images. It follows, then, that right-brain photographs are more subjective and often more abstract photographs, catering to the photographer's point of view rather than to someone else's particular demands. Right-brain photography, then, is devoted to suspending dictated logic, letting yourself sink into your senses, and letting your senses sink into new nonverbal ideas.

And there's been psychohistory analysis of Hitler as having a "very right-hemispheric temperament," and Stalin as "a left-hemispheric leader." And recall Beethoven, who was held to be illiterate, couldn't add, remember, etc. Beethoven biographer Jan Ehrenwald continues, "Beethoven's genius was presided over by the preponderant right hemisphere, while his shortcomings in the three R's were due to the left side of his brain lagging behind the right side in his intellectual functions. . . . Paradoxically, this state of affairs might have earned one of the greatest minds of his century a disconcertingly low IQ."

Further along the dichotomanic run was this statement, fairly typical of a generation of educators: "Students who do not find school very relevant could well be right-brain oriented. To them, the many left-brain tasks just do not make sense. There is also evidence that the urban poor tend to be right-hemisphere oriented, while middle-class persons are more left-hemisphere oriented. If this is true, it would explain why many urban poor do not succeed in our schools and why they claim irrelevancy of many of the tasks asked of them in school."

One high school English teacher stated that "there is little need to be concerned about the left-brain abilities of most individuals" and then got a wholehearted endorsement of television by the school principal as a right-brain substitute for reading. Innumerable authors tried to stimulate right-brain learning. Some advocated detailed programs of listening to music during lectures; looking at pictorial materials, televised programs, and videos; and creating individually tailored projects that related the information already learned.

For managers, one writer suggests that "one day a week, make it a rule that no one in the office or plant can use the word no. (The right hemisphere has no equivalent of no.) If something is not acceptable, the person must deal with it by saying, 'yes, if . . .'; give a 30-second explanation of something, and ask to guess what you're getting at." He is delighted that their new approach is now being included in computer software. This preceded Nancy Reagan's "Just Say No" by a few years.

"No" brain, no gain, I guess.

Other educators came up with a series of insight problems that would "unleash the right side of the brain" or form "mind maps," in which an entire thought sequence could be represented holistically in the right brain by a complex linking of ideas together via an illustrated format. The thought was that if the right hemisphere were stimulated properly, it would offset the traditional emphasis on the left-hemispheric three-R curriculum. This stimulated lots of half-thought-out analyses and good ideas for education or artistic work that hooked on to the world of brain research for no reason. There was an unfortunate run of right-brain everything, whole-grain–whole-brain everything, cooking, photography, history, alpha rhythms, and the like.

Although there's been a loosening of the academic view that "if you can't express it in language you don't know it," the explosive application of the two hemispheres to society has been mixed at best. While well-intentioned, many writers and educators depict complex thought processes as simple ones that can be localized *in toto* in either the left or right brain. One even said that some people "have such dominance of one hemisphere that the other hemisphere is rarely activated." This is foolish, since both hemispheres contribute to everything, but contribute differently.

In a scathing review, Lauren Harris wrote, "Aside from its misrepresentation of the neuropsychological evidence, its tendentious analysis of the school environment, and its aggressive promotion of various neuropsychological nostrums, there is something else that troubles me about the 'right-brain' movement . . . [the] attack [on] what they call 'left-brain education' in order to promote an educational philosophy and practice that celebrates or at least seeks to excuse anti-intellectualism, illiteracy, and irrationality. This attitude pervades much of the literature on right-brain education." And, unfortunately, for those of us who had hoped for some useful departures in education, this is about correct.

However, there are a few studies of value. The *International Journal of Neuroscience* described one in Singapore that involved 284 students from three achievement groups: normal, express, and special. The students were measured by the Cognitive Laterality Battery, developed out of Joseph Bogen's program, to assess the left- and right-hemisphere functions.

The high achievers *were* more activated in their left hemisphere. The low achievers were more so in their right hemisphere. Thus, a normal brain can have a different development of the two hemispheres, but it is most likely the effect of literacy developing the left hemisphere in the superior students, rather than a right-hemisphere superiority of the poor students.

Lay Ling Yeap, the author, concludes, "There is a need to recognize and to accept the fact that there are two equally valid methods of acting upon, processing, perceiving, and storing information. Instead of the traditional vertical dimension of who or what is better or worse on a performance test, a horizontal dimension on the relative performance between the two information process tasks needs to be accepted for comparison."

The conclusion is still too strong. Rather, I think that the left hemisphere is undeveloped in many students and both literacy and brain-based testing ought to be used to identify this deficit. The right-hemisphere specializations develop to their fullest when informed by a fully developed left side. Otherwise we get form without content.

After a quarter century, one must revise early ideas, *non?* Because there are more potential connections between the billion or so neurons in the human brain than there are atoms in the universe, it would be absurd to claim that all mental functions and disorders belong to one hemisphere or the other. The frontal lobes of both sides serve planning and organizing functions, the central areas subserve movement and bodily sensation, and the back of the brain controls vision. The lower centers of the brain govern rage and other basic emotions. There are specialized networks for transmuting waves in the air into sounds, and those sounds into Dire Straits or advice on how to fix your Chevy's muffler. However, atop all this, served by the great division between the two sides of the brain, are two ways of working with the world.

I'm not sure the explosion of interest in the two sides of the brain did as much good as it might have, except to give rise in some quarters to a freeing from rigidity. For many others it gave license to slack thinking and low-grade intellectual ability. There seems to be a confusion in assuming a right-brain dominance in individuals who simply lack normal education. The problem, to restate it, is that many educators looked longingly toward the uneducated as a model for a whole-brain learning and so confused the *lack* of left-hemisphere development with a *superior* right hemisphere. Certainly there are needed right-hemisphere skills left undeveloped in education, but this isn't an excuse for not developing left-hemisphere skills. There may well be something to the notion that there needs to be more right-brain development in schools, but understanding the essence of left-hemisphere and right-hemisphere abilities probably has to come before the application.

There's a popular view that the right hemisphere is reserved for special things like artistic creativity or amazing insights. The research since the 1970s shows, from the lowliest of molecules to the rat to ordinary thinking, that this side of the brain contributes to everything we do, and contributes an essential component.

However, the recent run of dichotomania should not obscure that the Jekyll-and-Hyde view of the right hemisphere as a dangerous automaton is not supported by the research either. We don't have our savior residing somewhere in the right hemisphere waiting to be revealed, nor do we have a moron living in there.

If there is an application to society, then we should have a better idea of what the sides really do. So I want to begin an analysis of this in the next section, which I sum up as the relationship between the text of written material and its wider meaning, or context. Both are necessary for full human thought.

Chapter 8

Wit or Half-Wit?

In the *Times*'s sprawling archives, the articles deliver the facts. It's the pictures that tell the story.

—*New York Times Sunday Magazine*, 1996

There are three people waiting, sitting on a bench. An older man. It looks like he has a bandage on his head. And the boy in the middle has his hands clenched in his lap. He's wearing blue shorts, white shoes with striped socks. And the man on the end of the bench is between the two of them in age. And he has a cigarette tray right by him. And he looks a little anxious. He's got his elbows on his knees. He's got his chin in his hand. He's wearing a khaki suit. The boy's wearing a short-sleeved shirt, blue shorts. The man's wearing a dark suit with a tie and the man has a bandage on his head.

—Patient with right-hemisphere damage, responding to a Norman Rockwell painting

I was talking with, or perhaps I should write that I was attempting to communicate with, Dean B., a forty-six-year-old Trinidadian who suffered a severe stroke in the middle artery of his left hemisphere. We were at the café of his London hospital. We had finished lunch and I got up to return to the ward, and for a second I forgot the situation I was in, what kind of patient Dean is, and even a sense of what was going on. I foolishly asked: "Do you want to drink something else?" He voiced, in his attempt to reply, "Ut, uta, des, des, des, der, ut."

I became embarrassed: Of course he couldn't answer me! Well, he couldn't reply in so many words but he still had a means to communicate with me. In response, Dean B. cupped his hands, pulled his left hand back and made a karate-like cut, moved one hand as if holding a half-sphere on to something and then moved his right hand as if he were pressing a lever. Then he put his hand as if around a glass and pretended to drink. Orange juice!

I said it and he smiled. He could do everything but speak the words. He knew what he wanted, how it was produced, how it was consumed. (And, being in hospital, I am sure he knew that it wouldn't be squeezed there.) And he knew what I was asking. He knew everything that was happening, but he just couldn't say anything.

He knew what I could do: Get the message, get the juice, and get it back to him. Like Dean B., other people whose left-hemisphere damage has left them with aphasia can use gestures, facial expressions, or tone of voice, grunts, etc., to request what they need. And when they are asked to do something, they respond in context. Make a normal request and they act, and they try to communicate a response in some way when you ask them a question. He had lost function of the left hemisphere and thus lost the text, but not the context, of his communication abilities.

While Dean's lack of text was literal, the relationship between the elements of communication and their organization affects all we do. *Context* is defined as a "weaving together." It is this joining information about who we are, what we can do, what our surroundings are, who is with us and what they can do and understand that determines our comprehension of where we are in the world, and in life. The individual words we speak, important though they are, are but the bare text that signs the details of life. Much of the recent research on language and the two sides of the brain provides surprising and important evidence that the two sides handle two very different portions of the world.

To get a taste of the situation, quickly read the following story, and then, before reading on, jot down what you remember of it.

> With hocked gems financing him, our hero bravely defied all scornful laughter that tried to prevent his scheme. "Your eyes deceive," he had said. "An egg, not a table, correctly typifies this unexplored planet." Now three sturdy sisters sought proof. Forging along, sometimes through calm vastness, yet more often very turbulent peaks and valleys, days became weeks as many doubters spread fearful rumors about the edge. At last from nowhere welcome winged creatures appeared, signifying momentous success.

You probably remembered little. When rereading the story as portraying Columbus's voyage to America, people remember much more. Having a context organizes information, making it more comprehensible and more memorable. A title usually announces an overall framework for events and makes part of what is read more accessible, as naming fruits aids recall of other fruits.

Because of context, we remember some events better than others. Although it is difficult to study how different people organize information into a meaningful memory, here is a demonstration of how changes in context affect memory. Read the following story once, and write down what you remember of it.

Watching a Peace March from the 40th Floor

The view was breathtaking. From the window one could see the crowd below. Everything looked extremely small from such a distance but the colorful costumes could still be seen. Everyone seemed to be moving in one direction in an orderly fashion, and there seemed to be little children as well as adults. The landing was gentle, and luckily the atmosphere was such that no special suits had to be worn. At first there was a great deal of activity. Later, when the speeches started, the crowd quieted down. The man with the television camera took many shots of the setting and the crowds. Everyone was very friendly and seemed glad when the music started.

What about the sentence: "The landing was gentle and luckily the atmosphere was such that no special suits had to be worn"? In one experiment, only 18 percent of the subjects recalled something about this sentence. Reread the story, but this time under the title "A Space Trip to an Uninhabited Planet." Now the sentence "The landing was gentle . . ." fits in and makes sense. Of those who read the story with this title, 53 percent recalled the sentence. With a different context recollection of this sentence is improved.

Many psychologists and linguists have until recently considered the text of speech as the only component of communication. But this myopic focus on the text ignores the essential context, which gives language its full meaning. The neglect of the contextual forest for the trees of the text is understandable: Words are right there before our eyes (and ears) and easy to study objectively.

However, all that we know isn't always available to speech; we need to draw or gesture to communicate fully. We produce facial expressions, differing tones of voice, accents, and changes of inflection to convey meaning. We also use speech indirectly, sarcastically, or in jokes. In short, the context of what's said is at least as vital to the communication as the text alone.

The text we hear can be meaningless out of context. Someone says, "This is great!" You have no idea what they mean without knowing the context—is it a situation that could be sarcastic? The right hemisphere decodes the external information that we use to compute context; it helps assemble the whole field of view to create an overall understanding of a scene. It helps us understand where we are figuratively, in terms of who we think we are, and literally, in space, in time, and in our field of vision. Of course, it has its own abilities to operate on the text of language as well.

The finding that has caused the most revision to the view that the right hemisphere is a mere appendage, or just a space processor, shows that the right hemisphere is deeply involved in complex language. My study in the late 1970s with Charles Swencionis of the Albert Einstein College of Medicine indicated that the right side engages while reading stories.

Recent work has dramatically changed the way we view the brain's handling of language. It's not only specially written material that involves the right hemisphere, for much of our normal speech is indirect. We often don't say what we literally mean. Even the meaning of an ordinary question like "Can you go to the store?" doesn't mean what it says. Its normal meaning is "I want you to go to the store," although the literal meaning is "Are you physically able at this moment to go to the store?" A direct response would be a simple yes, and no action, but this is usually seen as sarcastic. And there's so much in our speech that is indirect, such as "He has a broken heart" or "She lights up the room," and some standard parts of speech are themselves metaphors, like "The party platform," "They caved on that issue." Even the word "context" is itself a metaphor derived from weaving.

There are individual and cultural differences in speech directness. Americans and British are, as it is said, "divided by a common language," and one division is the way the same words are used. Americans are more direct and the British indirect, elliptical. I've had the occasion to sit with an American academic after his presentation to a British university, and listened to his British counterpart say, "I'm not sure I, or anyone here, will agree completely with absolutely everything the speaker has said, but we thank him for his trouble in coming here to attempt to make a difficult idea possibly more tenable to us."

The Brits in the audience almost gasped, but my friend smiled. He didn't get it. Later I asked him what he had thought had gone on and he said, "Of course no one would completely agree, that's to be expected." However, in the British this means, "I think this is a complete load of stupidity, and so should you." When I translated the message, my friend said, "Well, if he meant that, why didn't he just say it?"

Lots of what we say doesn't mean what it says. The intention of the speaker can be given explicitly by direct speech such as "Close the window!" However, this communication is not always explicit. Much of the time the speech act is indirect, such as "Is there a window that somebody has left wide open?" which is meant either to reprimand someone or to suggest that the listener should close the window. Or both.

Normally we don't notice how much work it takes to understand what's being said to us; it's so automatic. But it takes a few steps: First we have to know what is being said explicitly (i.e., a question about an open window). Then we have to interpret this literal meaning to grasp the figurative intent of the speaker. Even severe aphasics with left-brain damage, like Dean B., comprehend indirect requests.

One set of innovative studies presented filmed scenes containing indirect requests to five Broca's aphasics (left-brain damage) and five right-brain-damaged subjects. These people were asked to judge whether the response given by one of the actors was appropriate to indirect requests like "Could you pass the salt shaker?" or "Can you play tennis?" The Broca's aphasics, like Dean B., understood these expressions in their conventional meaning—an indirect request for an action to be performed by the listener. They could also judge whether the action following was correct or not.

Right-hemisphere-damaged subjects reacted differently. When considering two people sitting in a living room, one of whom asks, "Can you play tennis?" they think a scene is OK in which the listener responds by playing tennis, right there, in that living room. So people with right-hemisphere damage can always understand the literal meaning of a request, *but they cannot always judge what the request means in context.*

Picking up clues from the context is part of understanding whether the figurative or literal meaning of a word is appropriate. "Deep," for instance, has a literal meaning of "extending down," but it also has a figurative meaning, when applied to people, of "thoughtful" or "wise." People with right-hemisphere damage test poorly at picking up the figurative meanings of words.

When we listen and when we read, we attend selectively and fill in an enormous amount of information. The meaning of something causes us to complete the gaps in the elements of language, in the words and letters. As we read text, we are able to make good predictions the words we expect to see. These predictions, for example, were probably good enough to allow you to fill in the missing word "about" in the preceding sentence.

Our context influences what we hear. "I went to the new display last night" can get a shocked reaction from someone who heard "the nudist play," because the sounds are so similar. When I was very young, my father told me that the "Prince of Whales" was coming to the United States. I asked him for weeks if we could go to the aquarium to see this royal marine mammal. We use active processing to analyze specific sounds and language patterns and search for meaning. When the sounds are ambiguous or difficult to hear, we fill in the gaps.

People heard the following in an interesting study on this process: "It was found that the eel was on the _____ ." Different subjects were given four different words to end the sentence: axle, orange, shoe, and table. They were then asked to repeat what they had heard. Those who had heard "axle" recalled the sentence as "It was found that the wheel was on the axle." Those who had heard "orange" inserted "peel"; those who had heard "shoe" inserted "heel"; and those who had heard "table" inserted "meal." The subjects did not think that they were guessing the word; they actually heard the sentence as they reported it. Their language processors had filled in the sentence with the most likely element.

A long line of research has provided critical evidence that not only is the right hemisphere involved in knowing our place in the world, it is even involved in the way we describe our experience of life with that most left-hemispheric element of our mental world, speech. The work was stimulated initially by the late Norman Geschwind and instituted and encouraged by Howard Gardner (who has written much on the multiplicity of intelligence), with the collaboration of Hiram Brownell and others.

The use of metaphor, surprisingly, involves the right hemisphere. Metaphors, much like indirect language, sarcasm, or irony, convey a significance that is different from the literal meaning. In one of the first studies to demonstrate right-hemisphere involvement in metaphoric language, Ellen Winner and Howard Gardner asked different people to pick a picture that corresponds to a familiar figure of speech: "To have a heavy heart." The choice was between a picture of someone crying, someone stumbling under the great weight of the heart he is carrying, a heavy weight, and a heart. The results were very surprising. Non-brain-damaged people picked the crying picture four times more often than the literal one, while those with right-hemisphere damage split their choices evenly between the literal and metaphorical!

Many right-hemisphere patients also seem to have difficulty in summarizing the gist of passages. This is similar to their problems with metaphor, because a jump from the literal content of a passage to its overall meaning is difficult for them. And it's not only the essence of prose that they have trouble with; they don't get jokes either.

I am going to cite some of these important studies and use the exact material presented to right- and left-hemisphere-damaged patients. I warn you ahead of time, else you might question my taste in jokes!

You might well have heard this one, but don't stop reading, because it is a joke that was used in a study that distinguished which part of the listener's brain, if any, was damaged:

> A new housekeeper was accused of helping herself to her master's liquor.
>
> She told him, "I'll have you know, sir, I come from honest English parents. . . ."
>
> What might the punch line be? Here are three options. Pick the one you think fits best.
>
> 1. He said, "I'm not concerned with your English parents. What's worrying me is your Scotch extraction."
>
> 2. Then the housekeeper saw a mouse and jumped into her master's lap.
>
> 3. He said, "All the same the next time the liquor disappears you're fired."

Obviously the funny punch line is number one—if you are not brain damaged, that is. If, however, you had a lesion in the left hemisphere, you would be more likely to choose number two, the literal, somewhat childlike response, while those with damage on the right tend to favor number three, a more literal ending.

These peculiar preferences tell us a lot about the right hemisphere in understanding language. Punch line number three is the most logical here; it follows a set sequence and is easy to follow, as a standard warning to a fairly standard situation. With the right hemisphere out, the most predictable sequence is followed, because the text is understood but not the context.

Getting it, be it a joke or the point of a story, means having an overall perspective on what is happening. We find a joke funny when it brings together two or more unexpected associations. But these associations depend on the overall view and a sense of what's going on. Here, "Scotch" connects in most English-speaking people's minds to the "English parents" since both are terms describing subjects of Great Britain, and to the whiskey. "Extraction" also connects with "honest English parents" as a description of heritage, and with the making of whiskey, as well as the draining of the bottle. So "Scotch extraction" connects at several levels in the often unnoticed framework of meanings of the sentences of the joke, and this is what is mildly surprising and is what makes it funny.

Most of the time we don't think about jokes; we either laugh or don't, and the huge following that comedians can attract indicates that there is a pretty good agreement on what makes a joke work. But research shows that understanding a joke requires complex mental processing that we are not normally aware of.

There needs to be a connection in our hidden framework for a joke to be perceived as humorous. The first stage of joke processing is usually a mild surprise caused by an incongruity that slightly upsets our anticipation. The second stage consists of solving this incongruity by reinterpreting all of the information in a new context. The pleasure of a joke depends on the individual's ability to solve the incongruity, the joke being all the more funny or subtle as the level of complexity of the problem to be solved is greater. Not everybody gets the joke, no matter how intact their brains may be. Going to another country, or hearing a comedian from a different tradition, often leaves first-time listeners cold, since they don't have the same set of associations as the comic and the crowd.

This complexity that comes from the network of possible meanings of words is the province of the right side of the human brain. A long line of research shows that this hemisphere selects words very differently than the left does. The right hemisphere has an ability to hold lots of different meanings of a word available for use while, by contrast, the left hemisphere quickly selects a single meaning. People with damaged right hemispheres, then, have difficulty with jokes because they cannot hold the different meanings of a word or phrase in mind for comparison.

And there is ordinary humor in simple phrases with multiple word meanings. Double entendres are one such humor, and collections of unwittingly funny headlines such as these sent over the Internet are another. Here are a few making the rounds late in 1996:

> Prosecutor Releases Probe into Undersheriff
> British Left Waffles on Falkland Islands
> Man Struck by Lightning Faces Battery Charge
> Kids Make Nutritious Snacks
> Chef Throws His Heart into Helping Feed Needy
> Air Head Fired

And I once saw a sign in a restaurant that declared: "These tables are reserved for eating customers." I went to another eating place.

There are several different sorts of jokes, but to understand them you need to carry out the following procedures several times in a minute. First you have to follow the story, and as you are doing that you inevitably and unconsciously prepare your mind for what is going to happen. At the same time, however, you know that the punch line is going both to confound those expectations and also (and this is the important part) fit in with the story in a way that you hadn't expected. It's a sequence that comes out clearly in this joke that right-hemisphere patients do not seem to get:

> A woman went to a butcher to buy rabbit for a stew but the
> hares hanging at the butcher's are quite large. So, she says to
> the butcher, "I'd like to make some rabbit stew but these things
> are too big. Could you cut one in two for me?"

The joke is set up and you are trying to guess what is coming—maybe something about food or cooking. Then comes the punch line: "Sorry ma'am, we don't split hares here." At one level it makes logical sense but is not the least bit funny. However, when you get the connection between cutting hares in half and splitting hairs, it is (a little bit) funny. Your expectations have been disconfirmed but in a surprising way that also fits. The understanding of the fit is the domain of the right hemisphere, where different meanings for different contexts are kept in mind.

The trouble that people with right-hemisphere damage have with the punch lines of jokes illustrates another wider difficulty: They can't update their understanding in the light of new information. Suppose somebody said to you: "Sally brought pen and paper with her to meet the movie star." Immediately, and unconsciously, the sentence activates possibilities for what is going on, as any information usually does. You might first assume that Sally is looking for an autograph, which explains the pen and paper.

But, as often happens in normal conversation, the next sentence fleshes out the situation. "Her article is going to include famous people's opinions on nuclear power...." Now, with the new information, you might conclude that Sally is a journalist or a writer, and the pen and paper are tools of this kind of work. Knowing this, you most likely no longer believe that she's an autograph hound. Right-hemisphere patients, however, find it very difficult to process this sort of change, and when they retell the sequence, stick with their first, autograph hunter, interpretation.

Far from the notion of the right hemisphere as a moron, lower in capability than a chimpanzee, there is a growing realization that damage to the right brain produces problems with using and understanding language in normal day-to-day situations. Laboratory-type testing has been slow to pick up the deficits associated with right-brain damage because the problems are apt to show up in real-life situations. As many researchers in the field have now concluded, the role of the right hemisphere seems to involve maintaining the alternative meanings of ambiguous words in immediate memory, while the role of the left hemisphere is to focus on only one meaning. That right-hemisphere ability to hold alternatives underlies the complexity of our normal metaphoric speech, as well as our jokes. Far from a low-level function, the right hemisphere is involved in complex literary production.

Suppose you interview a man in a hospital with severe left-brain damage and ask him to tell you what he had been doing, his reply might run something like Dean B.'s: "Hi, low, if we'd gone through with it, might have, maybe have, done, then unlucky dormant." But if you asked him to use pictures and gestures to communicate, he might be able to let you know very clearly what was happening. One patient whom Howard Gardner interviewed was worried that the meeting would interrupt his therapy, which was due to start in fifteen minutes, showing his orientation to correct time, place, and social situation. Chances are that he would be neatly dressed and obviously alert and responsive.

Meeting someone with right-hemisphere damage, however, would be quite a different story. He would quite likely be a mess: shirt wrongly buttoned, hanging out of his dirty jeans; perhaps he might not have shaved the left side of his face, or if he did, not very well. His speech would be reasonably fluent, and if you gave him the logical and grammatical tests that completely faze left-hemisphere-damaged patients, such as "If the lion was killed by the tiger, which one was dead?" he would seem fine. However, he might not be able to see the left side of a drawing or of a clock. Gardner contributes other examples, as follows.*

When closely examining the right-hemisphere-damaged person, it would soon become apparent that something was wrong. For instance, if you asked "How long have you been here?" he might reply "Two minutes," missing the context, what you really meant, as he might describe the time he's been in the room rather than his total time in the hospital. Then he is likely to go off on a tangent and talk about something quite unrelated. Rather than worry about missing an appointment, it wouldn't be unusual for a nurse to have to come in and drag him off to it. Behavior like this would remind someone familiar with mental illness to think of some types of schizophrenia, a connection we will return to in the next chapter.

The bizarre behavior of Supreme Court Justice William O. Douglas after he suffered a right-hemisphere stroke shows what happens when the right brain isn't doing its job. He was paralyzed on the left side of the body, but in public he carried on as if he were fine. He quickly checked himself out of the hospital where he was having physiotherapy, told reporters his paralysis was caused by a fall, and when asked if he was fit to

---

*I am using "he" because the great majority of brain-damaged patients are men. This happens because men take more risks even in today's equal world, and while men do have more muscle strength, they are the weaker sex in terms of health. There is a fragility to masculinity that causes many different calamities to descend upon them. Males die at a greater rate at all ages, until there are so few left that the female death rate must ascend. It happens in the womb, too: 150 or so males are conceived for every 100 females, and only about 106 are born for every 100, and this is a gigantic biological difference, so it can't be our society that is solely at fault.

return to work quipped, "Walking has very little to do with the work of the court." But in court he dozed, asked irrelevant questions, and often rambled. He was forced eventually to resign, and his behavior became even more bizarre. He would insist on attending the court and carried on as if he was still a justice, having been unable to update the framework of his life.

Setting the scene is also very important to us in our daily communication. There's a big psychiatric convention in New York each year, and one year my wife and I happened to be in town. Since some of my best friends are psychiatrists, we arranged to meet a friend from Berkeley and two of his friends at the Village Vanguard to hear Bobby Hutcherson.

We began the introductions. I asked the psychiatrist accompanying my friend:

> "Where do you live?"
> "In England."
> "Where?"
> "In London."
> "Where in London?"
> "In the north."
> "Where?"
> "Do you know Highgate?"
> "Yes, where in Highgate?"
> "Southwood Lawn Road."
> "Great," I said. "We've stayed at a friend's house a block away, on Southwood Avenue."
> "At the top of the hill?" she asked.

As we got the picture the questions became very different.

So much of what we say depends upon an implicit context. If we were sitting in Highgate, a resident would be crazy to say that he lived in England. But in New York it would be similarly crazy to ask whether I lived near the top of the hill. Meeting in a jazz club in New York, the context was gone, neither of us were local, so it had to be introduced step by step.

So both halves of the brain are needed for the two elements of everyday language. The left side looks after the basic text, the conventional features of language: choice of words, syntax, and literal meaning. But taking part in a conversation requires a lot more than using the right words in the right order and knowing what individual sentences mean. To understand fully what someone is saying, you have to be able to interpret his or her tone of voice, apply the conventions of polite conversation, follow a narrative, understand gestures, and so on. You need to know when sentences don't have their usual function and be able to fathom the speaker's purpose.

This complexity and ambiguity contributes, too, to sarcasm and irony, and both are lost on the literal ear. If you tell a sarcastic story to people with right-hemisphere damage—"The boss asks the office boy to send off some urgent letters in the morning and catches him at four o'clock phoning friends, the letters still unposted. 'You have been working hard,' says the boss"— they are likely to try to come up with some account of why the boss was *pleased* with the boy.

Spotting the sarcasm involves being aware of the boss's real state of mind. Right-hemisphere-damaged patients aren't so good at this, and interpreting the words to mean the opposite of their literal sense seems to elude them. As we shall see, this is another major part of the background of our worldview.

What's missing in right-hemisphere damage is a considerable part of our daily understanding, the ability to grasp other people's state of mind, their emotions and intentions—hostile in the case of sarcasm. When asked about a vignette involving sarcasm, people with right-hemisphere damage often felt it was a mistake rather than a show of hostility.

This lack of a mental-state detector also makes it difficult for people with right-hemisphere damage to distinguish between a lie and a joke, probably because doing so involves making a judgment about what a speaker believes about the listener's belief. Take the situation where an employee phones in sick and then goes off to watch a football match. Unfortunately for him his boss sees him there. The next day the boss asks, "Are you feeling better?" and the man replies, "Yes, a day in bed did me good."

Whether the errant employee is telling a lie depends entirely on what he believes about the boss's belief. If he believes that the boss believed he was at home, then his reply is a lie, but if he believes the boss knows he wasn't at home, then the employee is making a weak joke to cover his embarrassment. Even though people with right-hemisphere damage understand that a liar expects to be believed and a joker doesn't, they still have a hard time telling who is lying and who is joking in stories like these.

The right hemisphere definitely plays a role in understanding what other people are thinking. Remember the finding that the left hemisphere of a split-brain patient, when confronted with an action governed by the right, simply made up a story about what had happened? Right-hemisphere damage seems to allow the left hemisphere to tell its own stories, whether they fit the context or not. When asked to say something specific about the emotional state or mental processes of a character in a story, people with right-hemisphere damage can readily produce a detailed narrative. The only problem is that the story they tell tends to be irrelevant to the actual story and the character.

Part of understanding others' experiences is interpreting nonverbal cues. When we speak, we supply some of the context by the faces we make and our tone of voice. We'd normally use these cues to help us understand the precise meaning of another's words. Individuals with right-hemisphere damage have trouble with nonverbal communication. Their speech is flat and expressionless, they almost completely stop using gestures, and they are poor at interpreting people's emotions from facial expression. Their poor ability to read faces might be connected to the general problem they have with interpreting other people's emotions or contextual cues. It is also possible that problems with spatial abilities caused by right-hemisphere damage could block the interpretation of any complex visual display, including the minute changes in facial coordinates that occur in facial expression. Accordingly, the way we understand the world, far from being a matter of the rational side alone, involves putting the different events in a life together, be they a discussion about where one lives, or whether a comment is to be taken at face value, or understanding "Can't anybody ever remember to serve the salt around here?"

Far from being Hyde and Jekyll, or the "save your whole life by getting into your right hemisphere to draw" views, the right hemisphere contributes, as Jürgen Lange said, not only in vision, but in every sentence we speak and hear, as well as everything we feel.

It gives us an overall view of the world.

Chapter 9

Minds in and out of Context:
Speculations on Some
Mental Disorders

The voices gathered behind me, keeping up a running
commentary on everything that was happening.

A nurse breezed through the day room on her way down
another hallway. "There goes the nurse," said a voice.

> —A schizophrenic patient, Carol North,
> *Welcome Silence,* 1986

*I can't tell. . . . I see one person here. . . . A doctor? I just guess
that. Here? I can't tell what they're doing.*

> —Patient with right-hemisphere damage,
> responding to a Norman Rockwell painting

If you were to look at a cube and experience it as a number of
disconnected straight lines and corners, you obviously would
not have gotten the picture. It is like perceiving that a furniture

kit shipped to you in individual pieces is the same thing as a finished sofa. "[Some] Assembly required" is what the package always says. Looking at the furniture kit, you need first to make sure that the individual pieces are OK, then that they fit together as precisely as the sentences of a syllogism do. However, you also need to grasp what the larger piece will be.

If you were to look at a scene like the one in our Norman Rockwell painting of the doctor's office, and you couldn't tell what it was, what the purpose of the room was, or why the people were waiting, then you might have difficulty deciding how to act, what to do. You might interpret the people there as hostile, ready for battle, or you thought they were watching a baseball game, as did one of the people we've cited. And what might you think of someone walking into the room with a scalpel? You might respond as you would when attacked.

We need a broad view of each situation to assemble the pieces of information from our lives. There's a lot of information to process, which we are normally unaware of: To live a productive life we need to maintain a sense of where we are; where other things are in relation to us; what the reigning emotional tone is; the nature of our current social situation; and how events, even sentences, relate to one another. Without these frameworks the world would be confusing at best, because the elements in any scene just wouldn't add up to a whole. The loss of context may make a person disconcerted, unable to know what's going on, and in extreme cases unable to act correspondingly.

We can sense the lack of context while reading about the Columbus ships and the peace march. Also, the odd choices of punch lines of right-brain patients demonstrates some misunderstandings generated by being able to understand the text but not having the context. In extreme cases, the lack of a broad view can get much more serious, so that the individual loses all sense of the real world and real events. And this can lead to serious mental and life disorders.

When we lack a higher-level perception, the world can seem to be a disconnected maze of individual experiences. Life's signs and designs are often indirect anyway; a sudden crimson flash in front of your eyes may indicate that your neighbor's car has arrived, and since he usually brings the kids home, you immediately register that your daughter is back from soccer. The same red flash could, however, be a sign of the devil's presence on earth, should your beliefs skew so.

So the human capacity to make up a sensible account about what's happening may run amok when our mental framework collapses. What I am going to do here is to present a different way of looking at some mental disorders, using the framework of this book. How might disturbances in the normal operation of the two hemispheres contribute to mental disorders?

I've begun chapters of this book with statements from people with right-hemisphere damage describing what they see looking at a painting that most of us find pretty easy to interpret. Their statements offer us a portrayal of the mind of the left hemisphere attempting by itself to make sense of a scene. It is able to identify and describe the individual elements well enough, but it lacks the ability to assemble the elements and integrate an idea of what's actually going on. Read again these descriptions:

> *. . . The family could be sitting, watching TV.*
>
> *. . . There are two brothers and a man. They appear to be looking at television. More appropriate, I should say, there are two men and a boy. All three seem seemingly looking at television. The man apparently is smoking because the ashtray is full of cigarette butts.*

. . . It could be a baseball game. They all seem so interested.

Boy scouts are sitting there again. I'd say something really exciting, but this isn't too exciting. I don't know what's happening. I see a guy sitting there. That's all. And an ashtray there. I don't know. He shouldn't be smoking around the boy scouts, that's for sure. If that's where he is. And then there's a little boy sitting at the end of that bench.

These two boys are—perhaps their father or their uncle has a bandage around his head—possibly returned from a war. They could be sitting in a church pew. . . . The boys have very serious thoughts on their minds. . . . I suppose wondering what their fate might be.

They're at the movies and they're watching a moving picture. Probably an action picture.

And this last one, that seems similar to the list of lines that the right-hemisphere patient drew to represent the cross.

There are three people waiting, sitting on a bench.

An older man.

It looks like he has a bandage on his head.

And the boy in the middle has his hands clenched in his lap.

He's wearing blue shorts, white shoes with striped socks.

And the man on the end of the bench is between the two of them in age.

And he has a cigarette tray right by him.

And he looks a little anxious.

He's got his elbows on his knees.

He's got his chin in his hand.

He's wearing a khaki suit.

The boy's wearing a short-sleeved shirt, blue shorts.

The man's wearing a dark suit with a tie and the man has a bandage on his head.

Most of us looking at the picture on page 140 would first say, "It's people waiting in a doctor's or hospital waiting room," and then we would describe further details. The right-hemisphere patients couldn't do this. Each patient's description has focused on one or two elements of the scene: people sitting in chairs, people with bandages, people with serious expressions. The last patient's statement on the list above has described in great detail the small elements in this scene, down to the clothes the people are wearing, but he is unable to see the big picture.

From rats to human beings, the mammalian nervous system views the disconnected pieces of life's puzzle in different size pieces. This distinction is not simple; it's not one side of the brain analyzing the parts and the other somehow grasping the whole. Rather, there's a precise and isolated meaning, what I am calling a basic text, to any message. There is also a larger view to interpret the text in. We don't somehow assemble three individual lines into a triangle, *but we change viewpoint and see the triangle as a whole.* The interpretation, as said, is often unconscious: "Bear right!" means something different in the woods than in the suburbs.

Seeing the large organization is a specialization of the right hemisphere. This principle applies whether we are assembling a triangle, a screenplay, or a scene from life. We can identify a wailing sound as a siren, and that siren as belonging to the police, but what does the arrival of a police car mean? Trouble at the shop? Dad is home? Your safecracking days are over?

We require the talents of both sides of the brain to put the world together, to know what your sister is thinking, or to know that your husband is mistaken about where the car is. We understand that a sarcastic tone, with stress on the "always" reverses the literal meaning of "She's *always* right, of course." While the text of the information and the exact words spoken may be handled adequately by the left hemisphere, without a right side to keep touch with the fundamental meaning, we're lost.

The world we live in from day to day is, for the most part, composed of other people, and what they think and feel has great consequence to us. Is he going to get angry? Does she like my presentation enough to buy? Is Mother happy? This necessary social intelligence normally develops in childhood. Here's a way it's tested: A small child sees his brother sit on the deck with a drum. The brother walks away and the mother brings the drum inside. The brother then returns to the deck. The small child is asked where will the brother look for the drum? As adults, we'd say that he will look for it on the deck, for we know that is where the brother thinks it is. A small child will say that the brother will look inside because that's where the drum *really* is.

The ability to judge what somebody else thinks, whether or not their thought is correct, develops in youth. This ability and other parts of social intelligence, like being able to judge tone of voice, understand facial expression, decode emotion, tell a joke from a lie, and grasp the true meaning of indirect statements, involve the special province of the right hemisphere. Let's look at a condition where the right hemisphere probably doesn't connect.

Autism is a devastating disorder that usually appears in early childhood and has multiple causes. Temple Grandin, a recovered autistic, cites sensory difficulties and problems with external stimulation as well as subcortical dysfunctions. Like all the disorders I will discuss, there are many different possible kinds of malfunctions in autism. But now, I'd like to canvass the situations where autism may in some parts involve a malfunction of the right hemisphere.

Autism's key symptoms are abnormal development of social and communication abilities, and lack of imagination and pretense in play. Autistic children tend to treat people as objects, and even treat body parts as if they were independent things. They usually don't look at people, although they notice great detail about their environments. They avoid eye contact, and often act very awkwardly and inappropriately. Despite these deficiencies in social development, autistic children can be quite competent and even have supernormal faculties with intellectual tasks such as calculations or puzzle solving.

Perhaps the social-developmental deficits of autism stem from failure of these children to possess mind-reading ability, the social intelligence to understand other minds. They can't predict what other people will do, don't know or don't care what their brothers, sister's friends, or family are thinking.

A part of autism may well involve a fault in the ability to understand what other people are thinking and feeling. Normal people, this analysis goes, have a specialized module in the brain, thought to be in the right hemisphere, for reading minds* that makes it possible to think things like "John believes it is raining," and to understand that while it isn't raining at that time, although John will still continue to act as if it is. He may put on a raincoat, for example.

This facility develops in children after infancy and contributes to a part of the fun of reading books while growing up. Children around four to five years of age enjoy stories involving these kinds of deceptions. For example, Snow White in the fairy tale does not know that the apple seller is her wicked stepmother. But the child who hears the story does know this, and also that Snow White is ignorant of her fate.

*Uta Frith, Alan Leslie, and Simon Baron-Cohen have proposed this and term it a "theory of mind mechanism" or ToMM.

Even earlier, at eighteen to twenty-four months, normal children start pretend play, which involves acting as if something were true while knowing it really isn't. And, at three to four, they can begin to deceive, knowing that other people can have false beliefs, hence the ability to say "I didn't do it!" when the child really did.

There is good evidence that attention mechanisms are deeply flawed in autism. Autistic children don't monitor, for instance, where other people are looking to see what others are interested in. They don't point to direct others' attention, and they don't bring things to show, to share an item of interest with another person.

Although autistic children know that if we receive something we want, we will be happy, they cannot "get" the more complex concept that if we receive something we want, but think we have not received it, then we will not be happy. The latter requires understanding of false beliefs. An autistic child usually doesn't understand that the child, in the earlier example, would think the drum is still outside although it is really inside.

It even seems that very many autistic individuals cannot reflect on their own mental processes, and may not even know they have a mind. If asked what the brain is for, they refer to behavior, "It makes you move"; while normals and those with other mental handicaps say it is for thinking, remembering, keeping things secret, etc.

In one experiment, children were asked questions about a rock painted like an egg. To the question "What does it look like?" a normal child would say "an egg," and so would an autistic child. But to the question "What is it really?" the autistics say quite often, "It is an egg." They apparently could not understand that they themselves could have false perceptions.

Compare this to the finding that right-hemisphere patients cannot update their understanding of a situation given new context.

In related research, Francesca Happe has studied the social intelligence of patients suffering right-hemisphere damage. As in autism, these patients could not ascribe correct mental states in a story comprehension test, or in cartoon interpretation tasks about mistaken beliefs and ignorance, or social conventions, impossibilities, and absurdities. Although she had few left-hemisphere-damaged patients to work with, she found that they did not have trouble with social intelligence. And normal people found the social intelligence tasks even easier than their control tasks, which goes to show how well trained we are in judging others.

There have been a few amazing findings in studies of social intelligence. Simon Baron-Cohen at Cambridge, England, and his collaborators in London, using brain scans found that an area in the right hemisphere is activated merely when a person is listening to words used to describe the mind, such as "think" and "imagine." We seem to develop the ability to learn to understand minds, and this shows up in the specialized way our brains respond to terms for mental events. We are born prepared to develop a knowledge of others' actions and intentions. Knowing what's going on around us, and what others' minds are doing, is vital to our sanity and our survival. And the right side of the brain contributes to these functions.

Consider what happens when one or more of these mechanisms of understanding life breaks down, or when they stop working together. What happens when there is a disconnection between the basic text of a situation and the context?

Alexithymia is Greek for "no word for emotions." This is a mental disorder in which a person has extreme difficulty in verbally expressing feelings and fantasies.* Alexithymia is thought to contribute to psychosomatic illness, alcoholism and drug addiction, post-traumatic stress disorder, and sociopathic personality. And this difficulty is present to a greater or lesser degree in many people who are healthy as well as ill. I think that most women consider it a pretty normal male condition. Attributes of alexithymia include not only an inability to verbalize feelings, but also a tendency to be confused by questions related to feelings, difficulty in handling feelings, limited ability to cry or to be impulsive, and a tendency to speak in a monotone and to adopt rigid postures.

Joseph Bogen, who did the original surgery for the split brains, and his colleagues interviewed twelve split-brain patients and found that both their dreaming and waking mental life were quite literal; their fantasies were unimaginative; their symbolizations were concrete, discursive, and rigid; and they scored high on a test used for alexithymia. The patients were particularly poor at fitting words to feelings and at engaging in fantasy.

These researchers then showed eight split-brain patients a short silent film that symbolized loss and death. First, a baby is seen playing in its crib, with teddy bears and dolls around him and above his head rotates a large white bird with black eyes. In the next shot, the crib is empty, the music slows, and the camera focuses on the white bird swinging over the empty cot.

Next, a small boy is seen on a swing in a park, then playing with a ball that he kicks out into the street. The boy runs after the ball, and a car is seen approaching as the ball rolls into the street. Then the street and playground are shown empty, and

---

*Though not a traditional category of disorder, interest in it has grown since the 1970s.

the camera focuses in on the empty slowing swing and the shadow beneath it.

In both little vignettes, the background piano music slows as the audience sees the empty crib or the empty swing, each intended to symbolize the death of a child. All the patients saw the film four times, and after each showing were asked to write about what they had seen. Even when specifically requested to identify symbolism or express feelings evoked by the films, the split-brain patients tended not to interpret or fantasize about the symbols and also tended to describe the events they saw rather than express their feelings about them.

What happened in these patients was a disconnection, in this case between the emotion-handling and linking of images to concepts that are talents of the right and the left brain. While emotional experience is not, in life, limited to one side of the brain, this deficit is clearly the result of communication between the hemispheres having been severed.

The split-brain people, because they have had an unnatural alteration of their brain structure, don't give us a complete representation of how the two sides of the intact human brain actually work. However, like everything biological, from height to skin color to hair color to verbal ability, individuals may differ in how well their hemispheres communicate. With extremes of variation, there may well be extremes of mental misfunctions, perhaps approaching the level of difficulty of the split-brain patients or those unfortunate victims of stroke or other brain damage who have difficulty functioning in the world because of harm to one or the other brain hemisphere.

Schizophrenia is one mental disorder in which problems with communication between the hemispheres or their balance of activity may be important. The very word *schizophrenia* is Greek for "split mind." However, this term refers to the minds of those with this illness that seem to be split from reality. (The popular notion of schizophrenia as multiple personality is completely wrong. Multiple-personality disorder is unrelated to schizophrenia.) Hyde-side thinkers have looked at the two sides of the brain in their fashion, viewing madness as a dominance of the primitive right hemisphere (what Henry Maudsley in the nineteenth century called the "brute brain within the man's") or a weakness of the more evolved left hemisphere.

The nature of the disturbance in certain schizophrenias suggests the opposite, that the overall worldview of the right hemisphere is lost. This leaves the interpretation of events to the left hemisphere alone, and as we have seen the left hemisphere alone generally makes a mess of reality, not seeing the whole picture. A decrease in the balance of input from the right hemisphere may happen in different ways: diminished activity of the right hemisphere itself, increased left-hemisphere activity, a lack of interhemispheric communication and cooperation, or a mix of all three.

Disordered communication between the hemispheres can lead to a disordered grasp of the meaning of things, and it is this change in the balance of the two sides' functions that I'd like to emphasize.

Some investigators, using PET scans to examine blood flow in the brain, found that schizophrenics tend to underuse their right hemispheres. In children, neurological and neuropsychological evidence of right-hemisphere deficits has been found to be associated with solitariness, "weirdness," and difficulties in emotional expression and interpersonal relationships.*

The research literature on brain and mental disorder is very mixed on this, and as we shall see there are several different

*S. Wolff, " 'Schizoid' personality in childhood and adult life, I: Vagaries of diagnostic labelling," *British Journal of Psychiatry* 159: 617.

subtypes of schizophrenia, probably each with a different pattern of disordered brain function. So, we cannot expect to explain all or even much of schizophrenia by comparing the two sides of the brain since the condition is too complex. Nevertheless, a lack of the normal right-hemispheric perception of the world is a conceivable mechanism for some of its mental malfunctions.

There is a romantic notion that schizophrenia is somehow a superior form of thought, and anyone who has spent time with schizophrenics can cite innumerable examples of insight, or unusual sensitivity or novelty of mind. However, to take a few of these unusual insights and assemble them into a view that the schizophrenic is a genius ignores the pain, the disorganization of thought, and the anguish these people live with.

Many people—scientists, literary and art critics, and others—confuse creativity and disordered thought. Each breaks context in its own way, but they aren't the same. The creative person, whether he puts a handlebar over a bicycle seat to look like a bull or a triangular chamber inside a tunnel to make an automobile engine that turns continuously, breaks the mold of thought. I once was talking to a schizophrenic looking at a fire engine and heard her say, "That red, it is a dead head, can burn the lead out of gas. The fi-red gas apologizes for the red." This could have been poetry of a modern kind, but more likely it was a set of associations limited to a set of verbal phonemes.

There *is* a similarity between schizophrenic thought and creative thought, but it is conceptual, not real. The conceptual similarity is that, in departing from the generally agreed-on context, new possibilities come to light. When thinking is released from demands of convention and practical demands, objects and events may be seen in strange and unexpected ways.

Thought that departs from accepted norms can be salutary or bracing or a breakthrough. However, getting back into the world of the rest of us is another matter, and without it thought can be simply disorganized, or organized on very simple grounds. It is interesting to note that among the relatives of schizophrenics are many highly creative people, perhaps indicating that a small amount of disorganized thought is very helpful but too much can cause severe problems.

In schizophrenia and other thought disorders, there's often a failure of the way speech is used to direct others' attention.* Schizophrenics have been quoted saying things like "We are already standing in the spiral under a hammer"; "Death will be awakened by the golden dagger"; or "I don't know what I am to do here, it must be the aim, that means to steal with the gentlemen." This leaves a listener completely in the dark about who is being addressed, what the intended time frame is, and what these phrases are referring to. Again, as one line of a modern novel or poem, maybe we could see similarities, but as the main line of speech we see that the context is simply gone.

Schizophrenics aren't good at identifying emotional intonations of speech or at conveying them themselves. John Cutting, an English psychiatrist whose work has been very helpful, found that schizophrenics tend to choose the literal meaning of a word over the usual usage. One of his patients read in a newspaper that "we must all be concerned with what is right in our lives," and became preoccupied with following all the activities of the neighbor who lived on his right. It's very much like the literal-mindedness of the right-hemisphere-damaged patient.

We're constantly establishing the identity of different sounds and voices. We tag a voice that belongs to our spouse,

*It's called the deictic aspect of speech, *deixis* deriving from the Greek word for "pointing."

another to our child, a third to a person we don't know but we never lose the tag of identification; even if we don't know who the person is we can follow one person's speech. We identify a person's characteristic voice by perceiving tone, intonation patterns, and the like. If you were to lose the ability to identify voices with these cues, then amongst the constant mingling of different voices, including your own internal voice, you might believe that a voice from afar is speaking in your head. Whether or not a sound is heard as a word is up to interpretation, too. It's not uncommon even for normal people to hear voices in the wind, and if contextual cues are gone, such events would be likely to happen more often than not.*

The shards of words we hear in the surroundings can become interpreted as voices from afar if we don't identify them as belonging to someone. And random visual stimuli, again without context, can also logically fit into other plausible organizations. Recall how the left hemisphere could make up stories to account for what it sees, hears, or reads, and how those stories had very little to do with the reality of the situation? Carol North, a woman who had a schizophrenic childhood and overcame it to become a psychiatrist later, writes of her consciousness during one of her days in hospital:

> After supper, I sat quietly in the day room trying to watch TV. The medication was slowing me down considerably, and even the simplest movement seemed to take forever.
>
> The voices gathered behind me, keeping up a running commentary on everything that was happening.
>
> A nurse breezed through the day room on her way down another hallway. "There goes the nurse," said a voice.
>
> A flash of light zoomed across the day room, burning out and disappearing into thin air. Had I really seen that?

---

*See John Cutting's *The Right Cerebral Hemisphere and Psychiatric Disorders* (Oxford: Oxford University Press, 1990).

"There goes another comet," said a voice.

Okay, I did see it. This could mean only one thing: further leakage of the Other Worlds into this world. The comet had been a sign.

"It's all right," Hal reassured me with his sugary voice. "We're here with you."

Interference Patterns began to materialize in the air. I stared at their colorful swirls, watching new patterns emerge in response to every sound in the room. . . .

Her ability to interpret individual events is certainly not less-ened! It's more the reverse, an overinterpretation of minor happenings. So the ability to organize specific issues is not af-fected (a mainly left-hemisphere activity). However, her ability to assemble the world's information into a single sensible framework is absent. I'm not suggesting a Laing-type interpre-tation that the schizophrenic is superior in understanding real-ity. My view is that the schizophrenic's overall framework for their life is damaged, and this allows the left-sided interpreter to go unchecked. Of course, there are instances when the schizophrenic is able to perceive something we are not. How-ever, in the balance, the lack of right-brain-type context build-ing causes great difficulty.

This is controversial, but schizophrenics tend to perform poorly at tasks known to involve the right hemisphere. I've already mentioned difficulty in decoding the emotions of other people, perceiving the meaning of the intonation in others' speech, understanding indirect meanings, as well as understanding metaphors and proverbs. They are worse than average on spatial skills, such as block design, object assem-bly, and picture arrangement. Schizophrenic patients, like right-hemisphere patients, have trouble "getting" jokes and proverbs and metaphors.

One of the standard parts of the Mini Mental Status Exam given to all patients suspected of psychiatric illness is a request to analyze the meaning of proverbs like "People who live in glass houses shouldn't throw stones." One kind of schizophrenic interpretation might be dead literal like "Don't throw things at glass, it might break and shatter."

Many schizophrenics and those with right-hemisphere damage have body-image distortions, sometimes feeling that they have fused with objects or even the whole universe. Another seeming right-hemisphere difficulty is the schizophrenic distortion of self-image. Usually there's some spatial dislocation of where things are happening, and where the person is, with the person's own thoughts coming out of others' mouths or television (called thought broadcasting). Properties such as personality are suddenly given a precise yet arbitrary location, such as the left knee.

Like right-hemisphere-damaged patients, schizophrenics don't have much success identifying out-of-focus or incomplete pictures of things. Nonetheless, they rush to give a name to them, even when the image is ambiguous enough even to make a normal person hesitate. Again, the rush to name could well be due to a heightened activation of the left hemisphere.*

Many schizophrenics seem to have an increase in left-hemisphere activity over the right, but this can come about in different ways. Some studies have found more electrical activity in the schizophrenic left hemisphere than normal, while many PET scans find normal levels of left-hemisphere blood flow, but diminished flow to the right hemisphere. And remember, schizophrenia is not a single disorder. Rather, it contains a

*The controversy in this area stems from problems with interpretation of this research. Much of it was done before the role of the right hemisphere in language and thought was known, so that it wasn't clear how to proceed in studying hemispheric imbalances in schizophrenia.

wide variety of syndromes, some of which have more or less of the left-hemisphere bias (or right-hemisphere weakness) or are unrelated.

A popular modern classification lists among the "positive" symptoms loose associations, hallucinations, delusions, bizarre behavior, increased speech, and thought disorders (e.g., derailment or tangentiality of speech, and clanging—stringing together words that rhyme). Some of the "negative" symptoms are flat affect, poverty of speech or speech content, blocking (inability to express thoughts), poor grooming, lack of motivation, anhedonia (lack of pleasure), social withdrawal, cognitive defects, and attention deficits.

In recent years, John Gruzelier and colleagues have characterized the "positive" as involved in difficulties with the use of language and "negative" with a nonspecific anxiety. They then showed a connection between the verbal deficits and left-hemisphere dysfunction, and the global anxiety and right-hemisphere dysfunction.*

Skin electrical resistance (electrodermal activity or ED) has been used for decades to study the cerebral laterality of schizophrenics. The ED responses are thought to originate from activity in the amygdala and hippocampus, parts of the limbic system, the brain's emotional center. Measuring ED response involves placing electrodes on the hands and measuring the changes in electrical activity on the skin occurring in response to a sensory event, usually a sound, referred to as the orienting stimulus.

---

*Gruzelier and his colleagues were following a line of inquiry begun in 1969 when Flor-Henry attempted to differentiate people with schizophrenia from those with other mental disorders and normal people on the basis of asymmetry between the hemispheres. Such studies did not produce any convincing evidence one way or the other regarding altered hemispheric lateralization in schizophrenics.

These orienting responses are larger on the hand opposite to a one-sided brain lesion. For example, if a patient had a lesion in the right brain, then the ED response in the left hand would be larger than that in the right hand. In people with undamaged brains, we would expect the larger orienting response in the hand on the same side as the dominant brain hemisphere. Using these assumptions, researchers interpret a larger right-hand response to mean a deficit in the functioning of the left hemisphere.

Larger left-hand responses, which are expected with more left- than right-brain hemisphere activity, accompanied the schizophrenia syndrome characterized by positive symptoms. These patients showed rapid thought, pressured speech, positive affect, and excess motor activity—things that are associated with an activated left hemisphere. In contrast, those whose right hands responded more to the stimulus demonstrated negative symptoms, such as social withdrawal, negative affect, and poverty of speech.

And if a group of schizophrenic patients was divided in two, one with greater skin resistance from the right hand, the other with greater response from the left hand, then the left-greater-than-right-hand response group turned out to have positive type symptoms, while the right-greater-than-left-hand responders had negative type symptoms.

In the next stage of research, Gruzelier and his colleagues separated schizophrenic patients into positive and negative groups with a rating scale based on symptoms. Positive-syndrome patients, expected to have right-hemisphere deficits, performed more poorly on tests of spatial memory than on tests of verbal memory. Likewise, the negative patients, expected to have diminished left-hemisphere function, showed poorer performance on verbal than spatial tests. So there is some evidence for different degrees of hemisphere dysfunction in this kind of thought disorder, some lack of context, some lack of an ordered sequence of thought.*

In dichotic listening, recall that a person is asked to respond when they hear a word or sound in the right or left ear while hearing things in both ears at once. Average right-handed people respond better to sounds presented to the right ear than to the left. Schizophrenics show this bias more than normal people, even when asked to focus on information coming to the left ear. (Sounds in one ear, remember, are analyzed mostly in the opposite side of the brain.)

Schizophrenics very often have difficulty sorting out the flow of incoming information. Some of this may be due to the way the hemispheres activate. Dennis O'Leary and his associates found that the blood-flow patterns of schizophrenics were abnormally lateralized during dichotic listening. In this experiment, both normal people and schizophrenics listened through earphones to environmental sounds (car horn); meaningless vocalizations made up of a consonant, vowel, and consonant ("xom"); and three-letter English words structured like the meaningless ones ("dog").

During complicated dichotic listening, the normals varied between right- and left-hemisphere dominance.† The schizophrenics activated subcortical structures on the left but not on

---

*A third set of symptoms includes hallucinations, particularly of voices in one's head, and delusions, such as the idea that one's thoughts are being broadcast to other people or from the television. This has come to be called the "Unreality Syndrome."

†While attending to the right ear for either target words or pseudowords, a larger volume was active in the subjects' left supratemporal gyri than in the right. In contrast, when the task required listening to the left ear and ignoring the right ear, normal subjects showed greater activity in the right supratemporal gyrus than the left. Also, when listening to environmental sounds while attending left, normals showed greater right than left supratemporal gyrus activity.

the right, and low blood flow to the right. Other investigators have found, like O'Leary and his colleagues, that normal processing of words activates both sides of important subcortical structures.

Remember, in a brain functioning normally, while the left hemisphere makes a rapid selection of a single meaning for a word, the right hemisphere keeps in mind a whole range of meanings associated with different situations. This is what allows a relevant interpretation of a word within the context of the current situation. Among other things, these variegated meanings is what makes jokes funny, connecting "Scotch" and inheritance for example.

In daily life, selecting the correct meaning out of many is important. Does hearing "Duck right now!" mean that you should try the canard à l'orange, get your head out of the way of somebody trying to slug you, or aim and fire your gun at a flying fowl? The findings of low right-hemisphere activation while listening suggest that schizophrenics might have difficulty choosing the correct interpretation of a word or a situation because of an insufficient contribution from the right hemisphere.

Many studies of schizophrenics' brains find lots of anomalies in blood flow as well as in metabolism and brain electrical activity. The simplest theory to explain all of the abnormalities is that there is a basic malfunction in deep, subcortical areas that control activity and attention and integrate the functions of the left and right hemispheres. Thus, the attention filter could be malfunctioning in schizophrenia, unable to tune out irrelevant information because it cannot properly manage the distribution of responsibilities to the two hemispheres.

One way that the out-of-context and -control view of oneself appears in schizophrenia is the recurrent self-image as an automaton, or more vividly as a machine controlled by another. Consider "Natalija," a schizophrenic patient discussed by Victor Tausk in 1919, who

> declares that for six and a half years she has been under the influence of an electrical machine made in Berlin. . . . It has the form of a human body, indeed, the patient's own form, though not in all details. . . . The trunk has the shape of a lid, resembling the lid of a coffin and is lined with silk or velvet. . . . She cannot see the head—she says that she is not sure about it and she does not know whether the machine bears her own head. . . . The outstanding fact about the machine is that it is being manipulated by someone in a certain manner, and everything that occurs to it happens also to her.

This sense of being lost while a larger system controls is unfortunately very common.

When some schizophrenics speak, they can sound as if they're focusing on left-hemisphere viewpoints. "My intellectual parts became the whole of me," said one schizophrenic man. Another schizophrenic attempted to understand how to interact socially by inspecting the details of other people's behavior, as if he were some kind of anthropologist. He tried to verbally systematize the steps involved in making friends and to devise "new schemata" for relationships on his hospital ward, and spoke of becoming a more efficient "communications machine." These, along with the "machine dream," seem to show a reliance on deduction and analysis when an overall look at the situation is required.

I'm not implying that we're close to a comprehensive understanding here, but separating out the different syndromes and identifying them with different hemisphere deficits is certainly a good step forward! There's much, much more work to be done in understanding the basis of different forms of mental disorder and their potential relationship to the balance of the two brains, whether the cause is genetic, environmental, or developmental. These considerations aside, there are a lot of clues in the literature directing us to look at several thought disorders, including not only schizophrenia but also perhaps autism, as involving a deficiency of the vital functions of the right hemisphere.

In brain injury to the right side, the left hemisphere carries on regardless, maintaining the status quo. It seems that it doesn't notice that the normal information coming from the other side of the brain is faulty or lacking. This could well contribute to the various disorders of awareness, such as not knowing that an arm can't move, or the common confabulation of the right-hemisphere patient, where the left hemisphere clearly has to make up reasons for behavior. Because it is the right hemisphere's role to represent the arrangement of the real world as closely as it can, right-hemisphere damage can mean loss of sense of reality—typical of the psychiatric condition of derealization.

Autism, alexithymia, and schizophrenia aren't all that goes wrong in the mind, and even these conditions aren't all right-hemispheric dysfunction alone, or inappropriate activation of the left hemisphere or lack of communication between the two hemispheres. There are scores of special-purpose modules in the brain, all of which can go wrong. Suppose you couldn't decode external sounds into language? In the final analysis, all these conditions are likely to be ways that the human brain can go awry. But now, it's clear that without the social context and real-world meaning provided by the right side of the human brain, serious mental problems can result.

From the early studies of the split brain through recent research on the whole, competently functioning brain, the scientific understanding has become increasingly certain of the right hemisphere's role in seeing the large view. The large view may include getting the point of a discussion; understanding the hidden connections to enjoy a joke; putting facial, tone of voice, and text information together to understand what another person intends; or creating and appreciating literature. When the basis of right-hemisphere function is disturbed, the overall view is also damaged. And this can, in extreme, take away the underpinnings of our mental life. With right-hemisphere damage, our ability to infer, to quickly grasp and to update our understanding of a situation, to understand what's happening and what we are meant to do, suffers and can make our thinking seriously disordered.

This is a very different view from attributing thought disorders to a weakness in the left side's activities or to a descent downward into the "beast within." Instead it notes that two major functions of the human mental system need to stay within the range of equilibrium. Normally, psychologists note a decrease in the normally high-level human faculties—such as intellectualization, abstraction, and analytical thought—that can indicate disorder, but the reverse can be true. Too much activation of the left hemisphere can result in an overinterpretation of isolated bits of reality, seeing patterns where there are none, hearing voices disconnected from the background framework of life.

It's clear, from this understanding of a few disorders, to the work on understanding metaphor, the gist of a message, the overall perception of something as simple as a cube, and even to left- and right-brain drawing and creativity, that neither side of the brain does anything on its own, and when one's "partner in life" is disordered, the other half, like a good friend, tries to take over. But neither can do the job without the other. We need the text of our life to be in context.

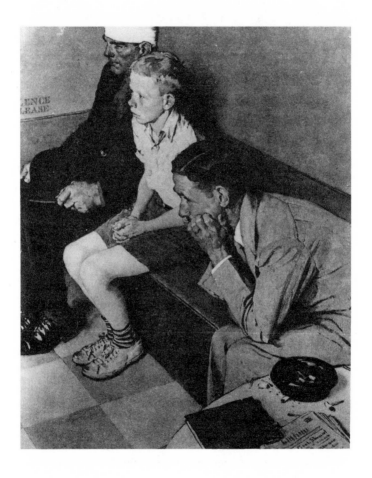

PART III

The Mechanics and the Music of the 'Spheres: A View to the Future

GLENDOWER: I can call spirits from the vasty deep.

HOTSPUR: Why, so can I, or so can any man; But will they come when you do call for them?

—William Shakespeare, *Henry IV, Part I,* act III, scene 1

The next chapter contemplates the working of the two-brain system in human beings and presents a new speculation concerning how the hemispheres develop along different lines and how they differ on their basic operations level.

Chapter 10

Making Waves: Furthermost Speculations on a Way the Hemispheres Operate

We see through a glass, darkly.

—Ingmar Bergman, 1959

Do you know that old movie cliché about the girl who takes her glasses off and is suddenly discovered as beautiful? Something similar happened to me just recently, except that when I took off my glasses one day, I saw the world differently and it caused me to think afresh about the relationship of the two sides of the brain.

I was a techie in my youth. I wanted to be an engineer or a physicist and, to complete the picture, I have always been cursed with bad eyesight, and so I've worn thick glasses, even from the first grade.* Being an unfulfilled engineer gave me the drive to present a model of the mechanics of the human mental system earlier in my career and stimulates me now to focus on why the different hemispheres should act differently.

Here's what has bothered me: Why should such diverse mental capacities "decide" to take up their residence into the different sides? We might be able to see why the left side should pair language and logical inference, but what of the positive feelings; the small hand, arm, leg, and mouth movements; the performing of high-level music? On the other side, why does the human brain place seeing shapes, understanding the gist of an argument, producing many alternative meanings of a sentence, and the expression of negative emotions alongside each other?

This engineering enigma became more troubling as I was beginning to do the research for the writing of this book. At that moment it seemed probable that the two sides of the brain were just a haphazard collection of special-purpose mechanisms for handling the different affairs of the world. You might translate the sudden cool air waves reaching your face and a flickering, sawtooth, black movement into an image of a hawk; you might interpret the downturns at the ends of your spouse's mouth as a scowl; you might interpret this information as the understanding that this signifies disapproval of the way the conversation is running too close to a discussion of your daughter; or you might analyze the sounds in the street to determine that the conversation behind you is in a language you don't understand. The amount of information processing needed to understand the

---

*I'm a psychologist because I decided that engineering and physics were too divorced from human affairs for me, and poetry was too imprecise, so psychology seemed to provide some measure of science and some measure of human experience.

complexity of our normal actions is one reason why research in artificial intelligence has had such a difficult time.

My engineering inclination and my bad eyes have finally led me to a different way of considering how the cerebral hemispheres work. I was brooding over the question for several days, sitting outside thinking about how the brain could place the different functions in the two different sides, and, as always, fiddling around with my glasses. I couldn't see how the systems got organized, other than just randomness. Then, pacing outside, fidgeting and rubbing my eyes, having taken off my glasses just to look at the trees, I got a vision of the way these great half brains might actually work.

I'm myopic, so the world loses its edges when I take off my glasses. Still, I can see the overall shape and the color of the objects in the world. If you are nearsighted, too, then just taking your glasses off will give you the same impression. If not, looking through a through-the-lens camera and getting it out of focus on the far side, or doing the same with binoculars, will show you the world in all its fuzziness. Or you can just smear some Vaseline on a window and look through it.

In this blurry world, you can still make out the general character of objects. I can. You can tell whether something is a tree or a face, or ascertain whether someone is blond or dark haired. You can see whether somebody's skin is light or dark, and can generally tell people, objects, and other things apart in a gross way.

We can see a general picture of the area, but with particularly bad vision (mine is, for the record, 20/70 in one eye and 20/200ish in the other) the details are a blur. Out of focus, one gets an overall view of the world, where the big things are, how they relate to one another, what their general shape is, and the like, but we don't see the fine details. Sound familiar? This overall view sounds like a description of the contribution of the right hemisphere, *non?*

I'm putting a lot of facts together in this chapter into one speculative story of the way the brain works. By nature, this story will be a little sketchy. However, in the ideas here may well be the beginnings of an account of how and why the brain divides its functions in the way it does. The story begins with the established differences of the cerebral hemispheres in other animals, amplified by circumstances of birth and growth in the surrounding world. And in us, small initial differences in our early years pave the way for larger ones later on.

In Diocles' time, remember, no one even knew that the brain was composed of different structures, let alone neurons. From a medieval conception that the brain is a simple, single edifice, different cortical and subcortical structures were discovered, and finally the building blocks, the billions of neurons, were discovered. No brain researcher would now confuse what goes on in the limbic system, the home of pretty set emotional feeding and mating reactions, with the more flexible actions of the cortex such as analyzing a shape to determine what it is. No one would confuse the thalamus's relaying of incoming signals to the different areas of the cortex with the areas high up in the brain that control movements like throwing.

When humanity evolved following other primates such as New World monkeys and the great apes, God didn't throw away all of her work each time one species emerged from another. As a result the neural structures that form the reptile's brain still exist in us, and in addition the brains of the fish, the cat, the rat, and the monkey show increasing complexity, but a line of development that we all share. That means that our mental apparatus is an amalgam of different structures evolved for different purposes, and coming to the fore in different eras of the earth's history, like a ramshackle house, where the old kitchen may now be an entryway.

The trend in contemporary cognitive neuroscience has been to identify these separate structures and works of the mind and project a mosaic view of the brain, different modules for recognizing faces, moving in space, decoding the air waves to parse them into the sounds of a lover, a poem, or a violin.

Many different psychologists have described the different talents of the brain, from John Guilford's analysis of 120 different skills based on psychological testing, to Robert Sternberg's few kinds of intelligence, to Howard Gardner's original seven and now eight frames of mind. I described many of the major ones in my *Multimind* thus: There are systems of activation, informing, smelling, feeling, moving, locating and identifying, organizing information, calculating, talking. And each could be broken down further, for instance, analyzing sound waves, or smells, or the rate of movement of an object seen in the foreground.

There's been a lot of controversy regarding these divisions of the mind. There's the question of whether there exists, in all these different systems, anything like a general intelligence, and if so, whether it differs between groups, such as men and women, whites and blacks. So, with so many different systems, it is difficult to figure out how the hemispheres could have perpetual differences.

Some of it happens through the amplification of early and small differences. A chaotic passage carries the hemispheres down different lines. To recap quickly, this passage begins well before the birth of an individual human being. It had early origins in the differences in molecules, of course, and developed into different systems of architecture in the rat, one better for looking at events all at once, the other for looking at each piece, in order. Animals that evolved later built on these differences, and the great growth of the human brain during its evolution allowed the hemispheres to diverge as well. But how does it operate?

Each time that a human baby is conceived its brain receives the great prize of our evolutionary inheritance. And, in each life, there is a developmental sequence that greatly amplifies the innate asymmetries in the fetus *in utero* and makes it human.* As a result, hemispheric asymmetry is not a matter, as the nineteenth-century ambidexteral culturists would have it, of different kinds of training, but develops naturally in the large majority of people.

The human brain is unlike others in that it develops much later in its owner's life than does the brain of other animals, so that the world of the infant literally forms the developmental environment. You have probably noted that puppies or kittens are ready at about two months to leave home and live on their own. How ready is a two-month-old human infant to do so, or one two years of age? (Or twenty years, one might sometimes wonder?)

It takes a particular amount and kind of environmental stimulation to develop the normal brain. Another cliché has the middle-class American tourist in Paris wondering how kids there can speak such perfect French when he has such a hard time with it. It's because the brain has organized itself around its early

*This hasn't always been so clear, as some eminent psychologists conceive that the hemispheres start out the same but differences develop due to the training and the circumstances of each individual life.

environment and, in a French infant, picks up the sounds and intonations of France, literally almost along with its mother's milk.

If you're not born into a language group, learning it later is much more difficult. I know; I once tried to learn Japanese and I came to hold the firm belief that it is a language that is impossible to learn, but there are lots of four-year-olds in Osaka who do it pretty well. And if a brain is deprived of critical visual sensations, as in experiments where vertical lines were denied, the brain learns to live without seeing them. This is the way that humanity, all over the world, has adapted to such different circumstances, like life in the Andes or the Dead Sea or Milwaukee. The human brain is the most responsive brain to what goes on in its outside world.

Because it develops late and in the early environment many different areas of the human brain are not on-line early in life, those areas that *are* on-line mature to deal with the needs of the moment. And this is how, at first, the hemispheres begin to develop differently. Bear with me.

The hemispheres branch off early in life, in ways that can be seen even in a brain scan of the fetus. The frontal regions of the right hemisphere develop well before the occipital ones of the left hemisphere. Early on *in utero* the brain turns in the skull. The left hemisphere twists back and the right hemisphere twists forward at 34 weeks. The infant takes up a position in the womb that often restricts its left hand, thus paving the way early for the right hand to dominate.

There's a real difference in the way the two sides of the brain carry on throughout their life: The right hemisphere matures more quickly and the left hemisphere runs faster. This difference, like throwing two boats into a river at different speeds, gives birth to their different directions, guided of course by genetic inheritance and the sequence of development. Making waves all the time.

So here's the speculation about a possible way the hemispheres would operate differently. Because the right hemisphere, particularly the frontal area, matures earlier, its functions develop earlier and in concert with what's happening in its world at the time. There is a delay in the left hemisphere's development near the Sylvian fissure, the area of the brain that is most involved with language. The neurons' complexity of interconnections with other neurons also develops later in the left hemisphere than in the right. But what is interesting is that these growth asymmetries may provide the basis for the later hemispheric asymmetries.

It is *when* the hemispheres become competent at dealing with the world that matters. A preview of the idea: The right hemisphere matures and becomes responsive to the effects of the outside world at the time in the infant's life when spatial abilities, such as finding the mother and control of the large limb movements, are getting wired up. These are obviously so necessary for survival. And the left hemisphere begins to become more and more mature, and comes on-line at that time, an era of life when the baby is exposed to spoken language and learning the more refined movements of infancy.

It's a fairly complicated situation, but the fetus is sensitive to what it receives from its tiny and restricted environment. Consider the brain's handling of sound waves. Before birth, low-frequency noises are in the environment of the fetus, such as the mother's (and the fetal) heartbeat, rumbles of digestion, and other internal sounds. It's very possible that since the right hemisphere matures earlier, it begins to deal with what's going on around it at that time, and settles in to understand the world through these nonlanguage noises. So the kinds of sounds that the fetus hears, combined with these differences in the rates of development of the hemispheres, develop the beginnings of hemispheric specialization. Again, a small difference early on . . .

I want to look more closely now at the situation that exists when each of the hemispheres matures, to see how that relates to how their specialization develops. I'll tour sight, sounds, which I've already begun to discuss, motion, and emotion. When you look at the developing human brain this way, through the timeline of development, a connection appears that was not obvious.

At the beginning of a life the right hemisphere is initially more responsive to the visual surround. As the visual system of newborns is not fully wired up either, and transmits indistinct and imprecise information to the brain, *the right hemisphere develops when it needs to manage these indistinct, fuzzy images. These are images conveyed by relatively low visual frequencies, just as low auditory frequencies are.* These frequencies yield information about the overall outlines of a figure as well as general landmarks of the features. This is what I saw when I took off my glasses.

Vision is our most dominant sense, and this is reflected in our own internal hardware, since more of the brain is devoted to processing vision than all the other senses put together. And I believe that in the long run it is the requirements of vision that drive the two sides of the brain apart.

An important difference is the way the hemispheres handle different frequencies of visual information in the world. Light waves divide into long and short frequencies. The longer frequencies convey the general outline of the figure; the short frequencies convey the local or the finer details. For instance, take a look at the photographs on the next page. The first has the normal detail of a face. Now look at the second photograph that

has the low-end frequencies all filtered out. You notice that, see-ing only the high frequencies, the general outlines of the face are still clearly visible.

The hemispheres handle these components differently; when a visual image blurs, the left hemisphere has difficulty perceiv-ing it, but not the right. Blurring the figure and removing the higher frequencies impair right-hemisphere functions. If you consider just the frequencies themselves, the right hemisphere is much quicker and much more accurate at detecting very large waves of visual information, whereas the left is much bet-ter at detecting the very short waves.

The right hemisphere of the brain seems to be specialized to analyze the low frequencies of visual perception that convey the general outlines of the figures. There is no way to get a picture of the high frequencies alone, but using the fine details one could easily tell whether something was a tree or a face. One could easily tell that two faces are different from one another by, say, nose shape or eye shape or some particular small range of details, such as distance between the eyes or hairline, but not perhaps by overall shape. It's also interesting to know that the same kinds of differences in frequencies seem to exist in hearing as well as in seeing.

Later in infancy the left hemisphere becomes more developed, and the images conveyed by the visual system are more detailed, so the left hemisphere gets to process information conveyed by relatively high visual frequencies—the low frequencies are like a fuzzy but general outline, the high ones convey the details.

All the baby really needs early in life is to be able to discriminate such things as the rough outline of the mother, not the fine details, like whether she's colored her hair or has a new face cream. So the right hemisphere, more advanced at the time of early infancy, plunges into the blurry view of the world early in life. This view consists of perceiving general shapes such as the mother's face. Then, as the left hemisphere matures, it is left to tackle the finer details of the local input. This specialization also means that the right hemisphere would be more likely than the left to deal with the information in the world conveyed by low-spatial frequencies of both vision and audition, and the left hemisphere by the high frequencies.

The large waves form the fundamental background images of our worldview, such as the overall view of the body in space. However, it's the small waves, the overtones in sound, that give the precision, the details, and the brilliance. The same thing might happen with perceiving faces.* This kind of development may well precede the right hemisphere's ability and superiority of the general shape for face processing and the left hemisphere's for details.

Auditory processing follows along the same lines. Based on its experiences *in utero* and as a newborn, the right hemisphere

*D. E. Schonen and Mathivet, 1989.

seems to "get" the low frequency sounds, and the left hemisphere also seems to become more highly specialized for handling the high auditory frequencies.

Because the right hemisphere seems to be specialized for hearing low tones, this very early ability may well lead to the later right-hemisphere dominance in a variety of nonlanguage sounds. The sounds of heartbeat, digestion, and internal movement are, of course, of relatively low tone. That this specialization lasts into childhood is shown by the fact that the left-ear (right hemisphere) advantage for low musical notes occurs much earlier than right-ear advantage for speech. Also, children understand and produce the emotional intonations of language, conveyed by tones, before they understand the content of the speech. The right hemisphere's role continues throughout life. In one study, adults were faster and more accurate judging low-frequency sounds presented to the right hemisphere and high-frequency sounds presented to the left hemisphere.

Given that small differences early on develop into large ones, the right hemisphere, taking up early "residence" for low tones, would continue to be responsive to the noises that it has been handling, and would be less available later on than the left hemisphere to deal with the sounds of speech. The right hemisphere's ability to deal with the low tones may make it also more likely to be responsive to the speaker's tone of voice, basic accent, and the stress the speaker gives to different words, which are all nonlinguistic aspects of linguistic communication. Later in the life of the newborn, as the left hemisphere becomes more developed, the brain hears the sounds of the mother's voice. Small differences make languages.

Consider our emotional life; again, prenatal asymmetries may initiate the adult asymmetry. The two hemispheres at birth have different emotions. The simplest judgment that infants make is whether anything is good or bad for them, whether an object or an event is positive or negative. When they feel something is positive, they attend to it; when they feel something is negative, they try to avoid it. These feelings also seem to be controlled by the frontal lobes, but differently in the left hemisphere and in the right. And they are present at birth.

This was shown in the study, discussed earlier, in which researchers gave newborns water or lemon juice while taping facial expression and found the same characteristic brain patterns that adults exhibit—that is, activation of the left hemisphere in response to pleasure, activation of the right in response to disgust.

While this is a further leap, probably of faith, what happens during the situation in early development might underlie the anger, disgust, rage, and other feelings that are handled by the right hemisphere. These negative emotions generally arise out of approach-avoidance situations, and one of the things that an infant needs to know very early is how to avoid situations that are dangerous, disgusting, or in some way injurious to the infant. Therefore, it makes sense that the earlier-developing right hemisphere might deal with these at the same time. Once the basic predominance is established in these hemispheres, the other functions may simply develop in the most likely area of the brain, just in the same way that cities are formed.

And there's more to this picture. It's very possible that growth spurts during childhood also provide a mechanism for the maturing of hemispheric differences. For example, during the period from three to six years, both frontal and occipital areas of the left hemisphere develop more rapidly than corresponding areas of the right hemisphere. This is the period that is also critical for the acquisition of grammar, an aspect of language for which the left hemisphere is usually dominant.

So the slightly later-developing left hemisphere seems to be more influenced by more complex information later on, such as the sounds of the mother's voice, the fine details of the visual world, the need for precise muscle movements, and getting accurate sensorimotor feedback. And again it could easily be that the two hemispheres may process information through different kinds of filters and that in some way the left hemisphere has tuned like a musical instrument to higher spatial and temporal frequencies and the right to slower ones.

In due course, in this speculative view, our two-hemisphere system gets organized handling the high and low frequencies. So the large dimensions giving us the basic outlines of vision, the fundamental tones heard, the large-muscle movements, are handled by the right side. And the left side deals with the individual details of vision, the auditory overtones, and the precise movements, like those needed to write and do surgery.*

Consequently, when the low-frequency waves of sight, sound, and motion are transmitted to the right side of most young brains, other elements probably cluster around, like immigrants settling together in a new city. And some settle because they are in the same cohort, having grown up at the same time, like the different emotions. As each grain of action comes together it is like setting up an avalanche in each brain as we grow up. The higher-level general organizing abilities, understanding the gist of a passage, simultaneous perception, and inductive reasoning, the ability to match shapes and tones, may well later settle down in the right hemisphere because of

---

*The same development could well underlie fine motor control and gross motor control. Early on, the motor system is not very good at producing precise movements and the feedback from making movements is likely to be extremely coarse.

the earlier settlements of infancy. And the primarily negative motions of infancy may be there for that reason as well in timing.*

This developmental view of the way the two sides get organized very strongly implies that the dichotomies of the '70s might now give way to a more sophisticated look at how the sides differ.

So I have changed my view in twenty-five years, but not from one where the hemispheres are different to one where they're just random boxes of miscellaneous tricks. I had held in the '70s that the difference was primarily between a sequential way of perceiving the world and a simultaneous way. In computing terms, this is very similar to the difference between serial or parallel processing. I held that these two modes would well underlie analysis and synthesis as ways of cognition.† The sequential left hemisphere would be good for analysis, and would underlie language and reason, and the right hemisphere would see things all at once, good for spatial perception, movement, and the like. But there was, then, no good way to see how all this analysis or synthesis could get wired up, or how wholes could be perceived, independent of the parts. Instead, now, we can see that the system divides into the large elements of perception and action and the small ones, and there's some reason to think that this could happen in the normal course of development.

---

*The left hemisphere, waking up later, wakes up into the need to handle verbal communication, to make small and more precise movements, and the like and probably provides a good home for tightly drawn inferences, as well as the positive emotions that go with small movements.

†I've dropped "holistic" since it has become a catchword for anything alternative, as in holistic health which is most often anything but, as it ignores the major developments of scientific medicine.

Of course this doesn't mean that it is all the environment or all the genes, and therefore one hemisphere is all positive or all negative, all thinking or all feeling, or the best way to perceive the world. It is a matter of the way they operate, one handling the larger fundamentals of sound and sight, in both cases through lower frequency waves (although this similarity in the wave forms across sight and sound may well be a coincidence meaning little) and the other handling the finer distinctions in language, logic, visual detail, and so forth.

Then, as we get more experienced, there can be a transition from one to the other. As a result the way the hemispheres handle the fundamental waves can differ due to life experiences, so that trained musicians recognize melodies better in the left hemisphere, whereas musically inexperienced listeners show a right-hemispheric advantage. In line with this, musicians show more EEG activation over the left hemisphere than over the right when they whistle a song, while nonmusicians show more activation over the right hemisphere.

However, the microsystem in the left hemisphere is certainly capable of creativity and leaps of insight. A point-to-point analysis allows us to check the world closely and to manipulate it with precision. So part of the final difference is that the distinction is not language versus nonlanguage, perception versus nonperception, or different senses connected to each side. Rather, it's an understanding of meaning, the small meaning of events and the overall meaning of a situation. We can't have the big meaning of things without the small; we can't have the reverse.

There's an important argument about whether there's any kind of controller at all in the mind and in consciousness. Does it run just like a crowded bus with no driver where the strongest element at the time just wrests the wheel away, or is there any sort of mechanism for control? Artificial intelligence analysts are trying to get rid of the idea, believing it to be a relic of our religious past.

I don't think this is a good idea at all, since it ignores all conscious control of our minds for an intellectual exercise. There is, I believe, an observing and executive function in the human mind. At the most basic level, we do seem to need the ability to choose which talent or course of actions to take in any given situation. This is what people both with right-hemisphere damage and with frontal-brain damage seem to lack. This is the ability to choose and maintain a course of action. And people with this deficit don't do too well in life. They're disorganized, incoherent, and make bad decisions. Recall the right-hemisphere-damaged patients who are unable to update their view of what's happening in the world, after hearing "Sally took a pen and paper to the interview."

I'd say that there exists in the right side a capacity that updates the different possibilities for action at any time. It's necessary, for the brain to guide us through this complex world, for the different centers of the brain to be put on-line when it's time to analyze sounds, update memory, or decode a new dish of food. So one aspect of the right side's overall or higher view of events is that it may well have a measure of influence over which mental module gets activated. Context, in our life, trumps text, not the other way around. "Higher consciousness" is another way of putting it.

Chapter 11

Restoring Context: Sounding Out Three New Notes

It is the night of Saturday, especially consecrated to a ritual which is awesome to us, faithfully followed by the devotees of a certain cult.

Two groups of twelve, dressed in colorful costumes, carry out complicated movements within an enclosed space. They at times respond to musical stimuli applied through a primitive instrument by a man of seeming authority who, with a few assistants, supervises their activity. Entirely surrounding the area devoted to the ritual, a congregation gives its responses. At times the people sing, sometimes they shout, sometimes they are silent. Some wield an instrument which gives forth a strange sound.

Much care has evidently gone into the planning of the geometrically designed arena. Around it are colorful insignia, flags, banners, decorations probably designed to raise the emotional pitch of the individual and the group. The atmosphere is eerie partly because of the abrupt changes in emotion. Their reaction to the ecstatogenic processes being enacted in their midst is so explosive at times that one wonders why they do not spill over into the sacred enclosure. Both joy and sorrow are manifested among the votaries.

This may appear similar to the Columbus story, or seem so confusing that you might have felt like a right-hemisphere-damaged patient trying to interpret it, or like one trying to understand Rockwell's *The Waiting Room.* However, this passage was written by one of the leading thinkers on spiritual life in the twentieth century to show the importance of understanding events in context, be they familiar rituals or the rites of an exotic spiritual tradition. So it's not only those concerned with the role of the hemispheres who try to bring things into context, but this function is explicit in the writings of the spiritual traditions.

The writer, Idries Shah, continues:

> We are observers at a floodlit association football game *[soccer to Americans].* What is missing from the observer's account is a knowledge of what is actually happening, and why. If we have this knowledge, we can identify the players, crowd, referee, the use of the chalked lines. If we do not, we continue: Here a man writhes on the ground, another grimaces, sweat pouring from his face. One of the audience strikes himself, another his neighbor. The totem rises into the air, and is hailed by an awesome roar from the assembly. . . . Then we see that blood has been shed.

This passage, taken as a whole, stimulates at least two thoughts. The first is that many unfamiliar rituals, especially those of other cultures and traditions, are difficult for us to understand unless we have the framework for them. The second is that this larger viewpoint on reality is what many of the seemingly exotic rituals offer. It isn't the kind of education we're normally involved in, the steady accumulation of facts, but a view of life from a different vantage point. I'll try to explain.

In the past several years, the idea of the capability of the human mind has been much expanded. Not all knowledge is spoken knowledge. Many forms of understanding, from representing space to knowing the taste of a particular coffee, don't connect well to talking about them. And many of the right hemisphere's skills bring an overall and unspoken framework or background to the human view of the world.

The higher-level skills of the mind are built up, as is everything in our brain and body, on the earlier, simpler systems. As a result, formal logic and inference have, as one important part of their cornerstone, the local sequential processing skills of the left hemisphere. What about the other side? There is a good bit of the brain devoted to knowing how the elements of the situations of life fit together, where we are in space and time, and where events fit into one another. So, is it unreasonable to think that these skills might also form the basis of "meaning large," the meaning of events in one's life? In this it would be perhaps the opposite of right-hemisphere damage.

The two sides handle the world differently, one focusing on the small elements of a worldview and linking them tightly together so they can be acted upon, produced, reproduced, like a formula. The other links together the large strokes of a life's portrait, where we are, where the parts fit, the context of our life. As a result, there is evidence that there is a special role for the right hemisphere in developing the overall meaning of many of life's situations: the large view, or a higher organization of events.

Think of experiencing the winter weather, first on the ground, braving storm after storm and experiencing the respite of small intervals between the snow, the slush, the rain, and the wind. Then consider another perspective on the same events, the view from a weather satellite, where the curved trails of the storms swirl into your area, and you can perceive that what might look like a sequence of individual storms are waves of one event.

And it's not superfluous to consider that there *is* a right-hemisphere component of the religious and spiritual attempts at understanding. Perhaps, like the football game, they may well be seen in a new, if cooler and more sober, light. If there's a metaphorical sixth sense of a different kind of awareness that one can develop, it is knowing about the relatedness of things, or, as Jürgen Lange said, the background of the human worldview.

Perhaps it can be thought of also as perceiving events and objects, like the storms, as a unity. What might from one viewpoint be a number of different entities, such as the disconnected corners of a cube or a number of people sitting together in a room with nothing to join their actions, can be seen as part of a larger whole with a shift of perception. It's a bit like the story of the elephant in the dark, where each viewer assumes he is seeing something different, but from a more organized perspective, the "pillar," the "hose," etc., are parts of a single, larger body.

The perception of meaning in language, like all perception, is complex and arises from a combination of specific elements and their organization. These greater meanings, indeed, involve many right-hemisphere functions. So we might well consider that systems that claim to help people find their place or the meaning of at least their own life, may well have developed, through millennia of experience, ways to stimulate this side of the brain to move forward to what we might call wisdom.

As a collection of bricks a building does not make, so a collection of bits of information, be it corners of a Maltese cross or the descriptions of the waiting room, do not meaning make. The microlevels of understanding are vital, as they are the building blocks of meaning, but they are incomplete. Perhaps this is a reason why some spiritual and philosophical systems describe their work as dealing with "higher" matters, which is based in perceiving isolated events as more organized, more coherent. Perhaps this more organized pattern-perception is one meaning in this context of being "wise."

In part, the misinterpretations in psychological science of the religious and spiritual traditions have been due to the precise nature of scientific inquiry and to a misperception of what spirituality means by training higher perceptions. An emphasis on activities of the right hemisphere, I submit, is the way many of the esoteric Christian, Jewish, Sufi, and other mystical traditions operate. They listen to low tones in chants, view spatial diagrams, puzzle over phrases that have no rational meaning, and attempt exercises to produce a state of "no conceptualizing while remaining fully awake."

This is why some of the techniques of the spiritual efforts are described as "not for your mind," or are held by others to be "anti-rational." The aim is the simulation of a new kind of mental configuration, as in the passage above, "understanding what is happening and why." Even the very different forms of meditation serve this purpose: They are nonverbal, or they use music, or they are movement oriented. The meditation method most often used consists of silently repeating or chanting a phrase over and over, or of concentrating on one object not only to become relaxed but also to turn off the normal internal talk, lessening the hold of the verbal mode.

You might well ask why I feel that I can discuss these issues regarding the right hemisphere when I have criticized biographers, photographers, artists, educators, and those scientists who have aspired to discuss their politics for overextending the basis for their analysis. Considering the spiritual traditions is valid because the religious and esoteric traditions are specifically mental-training systems. Further, their own descriptions show a concern with a lessening of the verbal and conceptual approach to the world and do seem to encourage factors that involve the right hemisphere. I don't think an essay on welfare recipients' mental states would satisfy these criteria.

The early mistakes made in trying to consider the relationship of the brain and spiritual tradition, and there were lots of them (due in large part to the excitement and the inevitably uneducated nature of early discovery), were too much identification with the culture of the '60s and not with what these major ways of knowing have always sought: a deepened framework for the meaning of life, and the meaning of one's life. This means that a special place is given to perceiving events in aggregate.

A research case in point: In addition to finding that reading stories written in the Sufi tradition stimulates the right hemisphere more than does other reading, my own research program found that mentally rotating figures by concentrating on their parts instead of looking at the whole uses the right hemisphere more.

But many began to identify spirituality with funny people doing funny things, and this was indeed fun for many. Young researchers, using the paradigm I introduced, traveled throughout the world attempting to measure the brains or the eye movements of mystics. But the excitement faded since whatever they thought mysticism or spirituality was did not show up on the brain waves. Thus the effort to find "EEG correlates of Zen masters" or other ways to automate a change of worldview failed, as they had to.

What I tried to do then was, as said earlier, to begin to open a way to a general understanding of what the different ways to higher knowledge of all cultures, including our own, might well mean to those trained to understand in purely rational and logical terms.

Much of what the genuine spiritual traditions—Christian, Muslim, esoteric—really teach is more like a skill, or a knack, knowing where we are in life, knowing what our role is, when to do what, when to be angry, when to allow our emotions full flow, when to suppress, when to use different parts of the mind. A sense of where we are and what to do,* an interest in a higher context, wisdom, or a framework for one's life is basic to these traditions and this extends into other areas of understanding, such as a different way to see the body and practice medicine. Consider this radical concept by the German sinologist Manfred Porkert:

> Chinese medicine, like other Chinese sciences, defines data
> on the basis of the inductive and synthetic mode of cognition.
> Inductivity corresponds to a logical link between two effective
> positions existing at the same time in different places in space.

---

*One could say, more strongly, that this kind of understanding relies on the basic operations of the right hemisphere which produces an integrated representation of where we are in space. But the associations have filled the culture. *Field and Stream* magazine even had an article called "The intuitiveness of the right side of the brain can be real handy come bird season."

> (Conversely, causality is the logical link between two effective
> positions given at different times at the same place in space.)
> In other words, effects based on positions that are separate in
> space yet simultaneous in time are mutually inductive and thus
> are called inductive effects.
>
> In Western science prior to the development of electrody-
> namics and nuclear physics (which are founded essentially on
> inductivity), the inductive nexus was limited to subordinate
> uses in protosciences such as astrology. Now Western man, as
> a consequence of two thousand years of intellectual tradition,
> persists in the habit of making causal connections first and
> inductive links, if at all, only as an afterthought. This habit
> must still be considered the biggest obstacle to an adequate
> appreciation of Chinese science in general and of Chinese
> medicine in particular.

Different forms of human thought may well develop from
the early differentiation of the two sides of the brain. Remember that V. L. Bianki showed that even in the rat the right side
was better at seeing links between things at the same time in
different places, and the left at links that follow in time in the
same place. These are two very different ways of looking at
the world.

The difference in ways of perceiving doesn't happen over-
night; rather, it develops in the chaotic manner from what is
present early on. Many of the higher levels of human thought
are based on the way the nervous system gets organized.
Nerve impulses, by way of illustration, do not respond directly
to the world; rather, they transmit changes in activity. Thus a
100-watt lightbulb does not send twice as many nerve impulses
to the brain as one emitting only half its luminance and does
not seem twice as bright as a 50-watt bulb.

And the wiring of our perception influences other calculations. If you are spending $1,000 for a sofa, you don't seem to

mind spending $49.95 for a new lamp base, but you'd think more closely about it if you hadn't spent the grand! This is because the mind, based on the older nerve circuits' way of operating, computes each new expense as a percentage of what is being spent, so the $49.95 might seem like nothing compared with the $1,000, but a lot when compared with nothing. A small light in the darkness seems like a lot, but at noon. . . .

In the passage I've quoted from his *Theoretical Foundations of Chinese Medicine,* Porkert comments in terms strikingly similar to Bianki's regarding the way the Chinese perception differs from the Western. Porkert's difficult-to-understand conception offers a different point of departure for examination. I'm certainly not going to argue that we should now drop causality or anything like that, but there might be an opening here toward integration and understanding of the ways that different cultures have come to organize reality. Instead of devaluing reason, or the framework of the world that the right hemisphere can provide, can we not try to combine the two modes? The aim could never be to return to a rustic, illiterate society with magic as the only means of explanation, but rather to understand what is really going on, and to try if possible to reap the benefits of different kinds of thought.

The aim in understanding different traditions and different cultures should no longer be to get a divorce from logic, science, and medicine, and hope for the angels to save us. Instead we should try to determine whether there are developments that our restricted scientific focus could embrace. It's not desirable to get rid of reason, but we could try to see how another perspective might help; not to get rid of science but to better appreciate its precise role in our lives. Instead of looking exclusively to alternative thought in health, the aim shouldn't be to get rid of scientific medicine but to see where another way of approaching health might assist us.

Clearly we don't have two brains, but one with a myriad of specializations inside, and two major ways of organizing the world. It isn't an either-or situation, or a left-right one. The ultimate objective of understanding the brain, at least this division, isn't a matter of "Drawing on the Right Side of the Brain," but of all the brain. One doesn't have to practice far-fetched (even though useful) exercises, travel to faraway countries, or try to reach far-out states of mind to involve the right hemisphere.

Rather, doing almost everything we do every day, we draw on the special contribution of the right side of the brain. But both sides are alive and well and are involved in all our activities.

It's clear from all the studies of brain damage that we use the right hemisphere for looking at the large configurations of a scene. So note again the way that the right-hemisphere damage affects the drawing of a Maltese cross, and how the right-hemisphere-damaged patients can't get the waiting room scene, although they can certainly recognize everything else.

In part, this interference of perception, be it language, interpreting a visual scene like the Rockwell, or knowing the identity of a speaker, means that the hemispheres don't seem to differ in the sensory mode of operation, but in the way each sense is organized. In this I differ from Howard Gardner's remark that the two sides of the brain differ in the senses they employ. It's not sensory modality—as there is so much evidence for right-hemisphere superiority in certain tasks using the tactile, kinesthetic, and auditory modalities—because to describe knowing the outlines of the world as spatial omits its musical and other auditory aspects, and it ignores the obvious need for spatial perception in the left-hemisphere act of reading.

This lack of perception of the whole configuration is, I believe, also relevant, but not in the right-brain learning manner, to educational concerns today. We're confronted with a large number of students and educators dissatisfied with the emphasis on drilling unrelated facts. Students lose interest, they don't see the relevance to their life, and teachers don't like it either. The Nobel Prize–winning physicist Murray Gell-Mann said,

> Since education is effective only insofar as it affects the working of the brain, we can see that an elementary school program narrowly restricted to reading, writing, and arithmetic will educate mainly one hemisphere, leaving half of an individual's high-level potential unschooled. Has our society tended to overemphasize the values of an analytical attitude, or even of logical reasoning?
>
> Perhaps in our educational system we lay too little emphasis on natural history. Perhaps in our schools and universities and throughout the whole battery of intelligence and achievement tests that we use, we do not seek out enough persons with talent to do the kind of work done by Mendeleyev and Darwin. . . . I would like to encourage our society to search for such people, and to support them.

The sentiments are admirable, but the sense is a throwback to dichotomanic days. I believe the question here should be "Does knowing that the overall perspective that one might need on events is the province of one side of the brain mean much to education theory?" I'd say it might help us focus on the role of connecting the student with the material to be learned, but otherwise, left-and-right-hemisphere education, I hope, will go the way of phlogiston.

Thinking about the areas left untaught was in the 1970s a useful concept to break the mold of education, but it succeeded only in chopping up the learning process. Two-brained learning doesn't have the relevance that many of us thought, except as a stimulus to action. We need to understand that the mind as a whole needs a lot of work.

The criticism that might well be made of how we teach and what we teach is twofold. First, the curriculum needs faster updating than we're doing, given the changes in the world both in content and media. I'll get to this in a moment. And second, there is far too little effort *connecting what is learned to the experience of the learner*—that is, putting the information in relevant context. "How much tape will I save," a friend asked me recently, "if I tape across the diagonal of these boxes instead of around the corners?" I suggested that he use the Pythagorean theorem and compute the length of the diagonal compared with the sum of the two sides. He said, "Is THAT what geometry was about?" Nobody ever told him that "the sum of the squares of the sides of a right triangle is equal to the square of the diagonal" could relate to his personal space. Without context the statement might as well be one of the voices in the street.

Math is a prime example of information that seems completely uprooted from a connection with life, and there is little reason for this to have happened. If there's no connection to the learner's experience, the information gets lost and becomes just another meaningless memorization ritual.

We should emphasize more of a top-down approach—for example, first teaching the overall framework of geography. Wouldn't it be so much better to teach where the student is, and where she might go, how the land relates to the people, including our own?

We're trained for drills and learning things without connecting them to the world. I always ask audiences to cite the months in order, then in alphabetical order. Try it. It's surprisingly difficult, to simply switch between two well-learned orderings of information. What we're not good at is switching.

Given the amount of information taught without context we don't need a special right-brain learning program, but simply to put the large picture first in front of the student.

Still, educating people to consider the overall view, or big picture of what is happening in the world, isn't a strong suit of our contemporary education and life. It should not go unnoticed that the kind of out-of-context information that students receive is part of a trend in society away from an organized framework for interpreting the world.

We might be tempted to identify this trend with the rise of modern civilization and technology, with people separated out into more and more islands of isolated expertise, lacking a general connection. It could be the loss of religion, stable communities, or of multiethnic and cultural life, the piecemeal information from the media, and the like, but this isn't a book of social criticism and it's beyond my competence to write one.

But it is a real problem; we are living in a world where more people are added each month than lived at the time of Christ, where more individuals have been added in sum to the world's population in the last 55 or so years than in all of human history beforehand.

The focus on short-term, close to ourselves, easily understandable aspects of the world is what certainly got our ancestors and us to an entirely different world. We've built a world that often overwhelms our mind's native ability to manage. So our focus needs to shift from the smaller ones toward understanding the nature of the larger systems in which we live.

The context of our lives has changed so much in the past century that it would be impossible to recapture any older framework. But the reliance on abstract and predominantly verbal approaches to the world has, I believe, reached a zenith, no matter how much we bookish people may decry it. A newer era of students no longer depends upon text alone; when information can now be conveyed via other means, the dominance of the book is lessened.

It is interesting that there has been a shift away from literacy, which has been considered the high point of education. In some senses reading is vital toward understanding the world, but will this always be so? Is literacy going to be as necessary in the future as it is now?

For 2,500 years, since the time of the Greek alphabet, the world has been represented to us in cold and abstract elements such as letters and numbers. Success in society often meant having developed superior analytic skills. There has been great advantage in codifying the knowledge of the nature of the world in this way. But literacy is one of many *means* to knowledge. It is not knowledge of the things themselves. I think we need to look at the new kinds of information technology as they might affect some of these questions.

While the written word isn't going to go away, and it has an unparalleled ability to convince, to illuminate, to train thought, to communicate information concisely, and even to stimulate, we might ask if it is always best. Is it better to read about a riot in Tasmania or to see it on television? Is it better to read about the performance of thirteenth-century music or to hear it on a CD? Is it better to read, even, about hotel accommodations in Paris or to see a video of the room and "move" down the street? In all these cases, the mode of more direct representation through multimedia has great advantages.

Students pick this up very quickly, and education has lagged behind the media available since television first appeared. Today, with multimedia applications students can gain access to information unavailable to even the most privileged people of a few years ago. And students' curiosity can be sated in many different venues, from Renaissance art to high-energy physics.

Soon, and for pennies, a few high-capacity CD-ROMs will carry the contents of a major resource like the New York Public Library or the Bodlean to any school in the world. But more importantly, being able to move through a web of knowledge allows the student to make sense of the information available in a way that texts alone could not, so perhaps we will return to a future in which a good bit of the lacking context can be provided through more direct representation. There would still be a role, if not a greater role, for teachers, but as guides to the meaning of the information available rather than as drill and practice supervisors.

The meaning of a situation is the arrangement of its components, such as the gist of an argument or the way the pieces of a puzzle fit together, so there are different levels of meaning in a situation. There are different levels in a society and there are different ones in a life. If not wisdom, there may well be a better balance between the text and the context of our daily lives.* It comes down to the meaning of the information that a student learns and the way he or she learns and recalls it. The research on the hemispheres may offer an important general perspective on factors that we need to consider in revamping education, but the research shouldn't be used to guide any specific program of one-brain-or-the-other learning.

So, to conclude this new wave look at the two sides of the brain, we've come a long way from the '70s. Instead of a fuzzy view of the right brain somehow seeing the big picture directly or perceiving wholes at a single bound, we have a view

---

*And while this may well be extreme, the lack of context has been cited by more than one writer as a key to both the increasing amount of mental disorder, and to the mainspring of much of modern art and writing, information ripped from its well-set place in society or in our minds.

of a fuzzy perception in the right side. I'm glad I take off my glasses often.

The right side doesn't (mystically) somehow perceive things whole, but seems to be specialized for the large elements of perception, the overall shapes of objects, the word shape, the information contained in the size, sounds, and intonation of words strung together. These convey emphases and much of the subtext and contextual meaning. It handles the large movements of the limbs, and the larger emotional reactions such as anger and disgust. And the left side handles the small, precise links that carry the smaller, more precise meanings and movements. It's this specialization that contributes to one side being good for the analysis of the small elements versus the synthesis or holistic vision, or language via the literal meaning versus the intonation and indirect meaning. I still like text and context.

Remember too, that the right brain keeps a number of multiple meanings, for instance of words, and this allows us to get jokes, or to understand the complexity of a poet's words, and on an ordinary level to respond to metaphor and indirection. However, when things are understood concretely, and it is time to settle on one meaning and "go into production," so to speak, then the left hemisphere seems to excel. Some learning, like music, most likely involves selecting one of the many alternatives and acting on it. Local and well-defined the left hemisphere's responsibility may be, but with that comes precision.

There are many lines of research that show that the right hemisphere seems to frame the small meaning components of the left and orchestrates them. When there is some damage to the right, it seems to leave the person lacking a sense of what's going on within himself or between the self and the world. This might well be some indication that a sense of meaning of the world in the large sense is what the right hemisphere provides, giving the overview of the person in her world.

If this "wave" view holds up about the way the two sides work (and I have no real idea whether it will or it won't), we get a complex but perhaps more realistic view of how and why our two great brains grow up to differ. And what each of them contributes to a whole human mind.

In the end, the question of who's running the show seems to depend on which of the shows we mean. Clearly for the point-to-point links between entities, be it strict logical analysis, or a surgeon's touch, or a writer's hand movement, or the precise movements of the human tongue, it is the left side of the human brain that provides the lead.

The right takes the baton when the large elements of the world need to govern what to do, such as seeing a familiar home or person, getting the gist of a speech, knowing when somebody is angry, and the like. It handles the components of the large view, as in the broad, fuzzy view of a scene. The right seems to provide the overall set or sets of alternatives from which to choose, the overall framework of the world, what's connected to what, what is possible here, what are the positions of the body, what are the possible meanings, and the like.

If we take a modern view that the mind is made up of different talents, each of them on stage at any time, then it is clearly the right hemisphere that provides this stage. And given the right hemisphere's focus on the large elements of our lives, it provides the possibilities for us to choose, by a complex process involving all the brain's power, what we might call "the right mind" for different situations.

Notes

---

p. 49   **Diseases of this type:** The quote continues:

In 1806, the famous naturalist Broussonnet lost his memory for words
after an attack of apoplexy. He lived for about a year after this attack,
but his residence in a city far from where I live deprived me for a long
time of some ideas which would have provided me with the history of
his illness and the details of the autopsy. In 1809, I made a third observation on the forgetting of words in a man suffering from a cancer of
the face, from which he died a few months after my visit.

These three examples were without connection for me and taught
me nothing until I had occasion to read Cuvier's eulogy of Broussonnet
in 1811. Here I noted, among other things, that a large ulcer on the left
side of the brain had been found. Immediately, my thinking went back
to the subject of my first observation, who had been wounded on the
left side; and, as for the third, I recalled very clearly that the cancerous
tumor was on the left half of the face.

. . . At the end of 1812 a fourth observation, and a fifth at the beginning of 1813, gave me hope of being able to convert my first observations into a general rule. This hope was conspicuously confirmed by a
sixth example in 1814. . . .

p. 53 **A double animal:** A. L. Wigan, *The Duality of the Mind. Proved by the Structure, Functions, and Diseases of the Brain, and by the Phenomena of Mental Derangement, and shewn to be essential to moral responsibility* (London: Longman, Brown, Green and Longmans, 1844).

p. 53 **One brain affecting another:** Generally, for Wigan, disease of one brain is a cause of conscious delusion.

p. 54 **Jekyll & Hyde:** The "Jekyll and Hyde" cases attracted considerable attention until the early part of the twentieth century, the interest capped in Morton Prince's book *The Dissociation of Personality* (1906), a study of a charming Miss Beauchamp who occasionally appeared to adopt the personality of an altogether different, and much darker, person known as Sally B.

p. 56 **Two powerful hands:** Quoted in John Jackson, *Ambidexterity* (London: Kegan Paul, Trench, Trübner & Co., 1905), 248–50.

p. 56 **Better brain, better thought:** In J. L. Tadd, *New Methods in Education: Art, Manual Training, Nature Study* (London: Orange Judd, 1899).

p. 57 **Ambidexterity movement:** G. Gould, "The Origin of Right-Handedness," *Boston Medical and Surgical Journal* 157, no. 18 (1907): 597–601.

p. 57 **Bend sinister:** J. Crichton-Browne, "Dexterity and the Bend Sinister," lecture given 3 May 1907 to the Royal Institution of Great Britain.

p. 60 **General background:** J. Lange, "Agnosien und Apraxien," in *Handbuch der Neurologie,* 6 Band, ed. O. Bumke and O. Foerster (Berlin: Springer, 1936). His studies showed that the right hemisphere is responsible for the general construction of the perceived background, whereas the left hemisphere is responsible for the more separated and distinguished objects in the foreground.

p. 63 **Geschwind:** N. Geschwind, "Disorders of higher cortical function in children," *Clinical Proceedings of the Children's Hospital* 28 (1972): 261–72.

p. 89 **Differences between the traditions:** Hopi language was held to be more involved with perceptual field, so that speech was linked immediately with its context, in contrast to English, which separates the user from the perceptual field. Therefore, there should be more right-brain activity when bilingual Hopi children listen to a story in Hopi than in English. Likewise, the Navajo culture and language (said to be more literal and concrete than English) made the Navajo's *thought* itself more "apperceptive"—more in tune with spatial environment so more "right-hemispheric."

p. 93 **Looking at TV:** M. P. Grady and E. A. Luecke, *Education and the Brain* (Bloomington, Ind.: Phi Delta Kappa Educational Foundation, 1978).

p. 95 **Lay Ling Yeap:** Lay Ling Yeap, "V: Hemisphericity and Student Achievement," *International Journal of Neuroscience* 48, no. 3–4 (1989): 225–32.

p. 99 **With hocked gems:** D. J. Dooling and R. Lachman (1971), "Effects of comprehension on retention of prose," *Journal of Experimental Psychology* 88, 216–22.

p. 100 **Peace march:** J. D. Bransford and M. K. Johnson (1974), "Contextual prerequisites for understanding. Some investigations of comprehension and recall," *Journal of Verbal Learning and Verbal Behavior* 11, 717–26.

p. 103 **Dean B.:** Broca even had some doubts, as in his paper of 1865 he asserted that the left hemispheric was dominant for articulate speech. But

This does not mean to say that the left hemisphere is the exclusive center of the general capacity of language, which consists of establishing a determined relationship between an idea and a sign, nor even of the special capacity of articulate speech, which consists of establishing a determined relationship between an idea and an articulate word. The right hemisphere is not more than a stranger than the left hemisphere to this special faculty, and the proof is that the person rendered speech disabled through a deep and extensive lesion of the left hemisphere is, in general, deprived only of the faculty to reproduce the sounds of articulate speech; he understands perfectly the connection between ideas and words. In other words, the capacity to conceive these connections belongs to both hemispheres, and these can, in the case of a malady, reciprocally substitute for each other; however, the faculty to express them by means of coordinated movements in which the practice requires a very long period of training, appears to belong to but one hemisphere, which is almost always the left hemisphere.

p. 129 **Schizophrenics:** If asked to choose which of the words *warm, cold,* and *hateful* go best together, schizophrenics choose *cold* and *warm,* whereas most of us choose *cold* and *hateful,* the words that have a shared metaphorical and human association, as do right-hemisphere-damaged patients. And I and others who have spent time with right-hemisphere-damaged patients' speech have noticed that their conversation seems more than a bit schizophrenic.

Many acutely ill schizophrenics cannot recognize facial impressions properly. They have difficulty understanding the intonations and the identification of speakers. As in right-hemisphere damage, the first part of the process works, so they can get the literal meaning. However, since the emotional or implied meaning required for the second stage of understanding is lost, their more limited left-side interpreter seems to pick a literal meaning at random. They cannot use knowledge of the speaker's state of mind (conveyed by intonation, place, time, and other forms of context) to decide which meaning is best.

p. 131 **Carol North:** She goes on to say,

When the voices spoke, the patterns shifted, just as they did with other sounds. It was like the vampire test: vampires don't have reflections in mirrors; nonexistent voices shouldn't affect the patterns the way other sounds did. That was scientific proof that the voices were just as real as everything else in the world; actually they seemed even more real.

Frightening. I didn't know whether existence in the Other World would be divinely magnificent, beyond human description, like heaven, or whether it would be like the worst imaginable hell. I was ambivalent about whether I wanted it to happen. On one hand, I didn't want to stop the emergence of goodness, yet if it threatened to be hellish, I would have to try to prevent it. I froze, not wanting to produce further patterns from the stimulation of my bodily movement. I didn't want to be responsible for encouraging such change in the world. Live your life as a prayer, I reminded myself. I heard a news announcer on TV parrot my words: "Live your life as a prayer."

Yes, that was good advice for the world to know. The newscaster had broadcast my own thought. The communication systems brought in from the Other Worlds were incredibly sophisticated, more than I could understand. The whole world was now praying with me. A nurse sat down next to me on the couch and put her hand on my arm. "Carol, what's going on with you? You're just sitting there doing nothing. Are you bored?"

The sound of her voice created new waves of Interference Patterns, sent hurtling through the air in front of us. Hush! Don't you understand what you're doing? For God's sake, don't help the Other Side.

She shook my arm gently. "Why, Carol, I believe you look scared. Am I right?" Oh, no, now you've done it, you've inadvertently hurled us into that bottomless pit. With the force of your movement you've made us start to fall again.

The nurse got up and went for help. She returned with two male aides, who picked me up off the couch, carried me to my bed, and left me lying there alone in the dark. The whole time, the patterns swirled through the air, crashing over my head like a tidal wave. Would any of us survive this ordeal?

On my bed, undisturbed, unmoving, I applied the powers of my concentration, gradually settling the turbulent waters of the Other Side. The Interference Patterns began to fade back into the air. If I could only lie still indefinitely, I might have a chance.

—Carol North, *Welcome Silence* (New York: Simon & Schuster, 1987).

p.132 **The rush to name:** Medication can affect the results. For instance, in PET scans using radioactive glucose researcher Reuven Gur found higher metabolism in the left than right hemispheres of unmedicated schizophrenics. This asymmetry disappeared after several weeks of neuroleptic (antipsychotic drug) therapy, and resultant clinical improvement. Studies done without this in mind, using medicated patients, would be expected to find less hemispheric asymmetry.

This distinction has a long history. John Hughlings-Jackson, who had prophetic ideas concerning the role of the hemispheres, also concluded that there are different levels of functioning in the nervous system and they affect the person's perception of the world. The insane person in his view would have "a lower consciousness and a shallower nervous system than the former person, his sane self." Mental disorder would then be a consequence of a disintegration of the consciously controlled mental processes.

The effects of this disintegration, he argued, could show up in one of two ways: either directly, as "negative" mental symptoms, involving deficiencies of higher mental processes such as volition, control, consciousness, and reasoning, or more indirectly, in the form of "positive" symptoms such as hallucinations, delusions, or impulsive and automatic behavior patterns. Jackson viewed the positive symptoms as emerging from "lower" or more primitive levels of the nervous system that had been released due to the failure of the higher levels to exert control.

p. 133 **Gruzelier:** J. Gruzelier and A. Raine, "Bilateral electrodermal activity and cerebral mechanisms in syndromes of schizophrenia and the schizotypal personality," *International Journal of Psychophysiology* 16 (1994): 1–16. J. Gruzelier, "Syndromes of schizophrenia and schizotypy, hemispheric imbalance and sex differences: implications for developmental psychopathology," *International Journal of Psychophysiology* 16 (1994): 167–78.

p. 134 **Poverty of speech:** Thus, three syndromes of schizophrenia have been identified: positive, with left-brain bias; negative, with right-brain bias; and unreality, which hasn't been clearly linked to either hemisphere. However, given what we know about the right hemisphere orienting us in the world, it would not be surprising if it turned out that some disconnection between the left and right hemispheres was involved. In any case, the three syndromes are not mutually exclusive; one patient can exhibit features of more than one syndrome.

However, the origin of the asymmetries of schizophrenia remains unknown. There are many places where they could arise, from brain stem to thalamus to cortex to the connections between the cortices. As a consequence of these findings, the two syndromes had been dubbed "active" (positive symptoms, left hemisphere more active) and "withdrawn" (negative symptoms, right hemisphere more active). The term "active" was chosen to describe the positive symptom syndrome because "activation appeared to be the basic underlying feature that distinguished the Active/Withdrawn syndromes" (Gruzelier, ibid.)

p. 137 **My intellectual parts:** Quoted in R. Rosser, "The psychopathology of thinking and feeling in a schizophrenic," *International Journal of Psychoanalysis* 60 (1979): 182.

p. 154 **High and low frequencies:** The right hemisphere might then become "awake" so to speak at the time when these coarse movements are all the system can deal with. And like a city first settled by one particular group, once it gets the territory, the left hemisphere may take over what's left, in this case the finer motor movements. The time when the right hemisphere becomes active earlier is when the motor system is very jerky and can't produce fine control, but the awkward grasping and reaching of the infant. When the left comes on board, the child can grasp cups, move hands in a more refined manner, and it takes control.

And there's probably some genetic bias to this, as the left forelimb in many animals is often used for grasping and reaching while the right is more often used for fine manipulation. In a right-handed person, the two hands most often work together in the same kind of movement relationship as do the hemispheres in vision and hearing. In a right-handed individual the right hand tends to make the smaller, faster, more high-precision movements such as in writing, and the left hand makes the slower, larger movements such as moving the paper, balancing the paper, and keeping the person upright. The same thing tends to happen in sewing as well as in ordinary home repair. If you're right-handed, think of how you sew, or hammer a nail. The left hand makes the slower, larger movements, and the right hand the finer, faster ones.

p. 166 **Ways to higher knowledge:** I'm not trying in this book to resuscitate the mistakes and overenthusiastic responses of many, but neither do I want a more comprehensive view of human attempts to understand the world to again be discarded.

Selected References

Akelaitis, A. J. 1944. A study of gnosis, praxis, and language following section of the corpus callosum and anterior commissure. *J. Neurosurg.* 1: 94–102.

———. 1988. Brain imaging: Applications in psychiatry. *Science* 239: 1381.

———. 1984. *The Broken Brain: The Biological Revolution in Psychiatry.* New York: Harper & Row.

Annett, M. 1967. The binomial distribution of right, mixed, and left handedness. *Q. J. Exp. Psychol.* 19: 327–33.

———. 1981. The genetics of handedness. *Trends in Neurosci.* 4: 256–58.

Aoki, C. 1990. Hemispheric lateralization of Japanese kanjin and kana: Evidence for right hemisphere involvement in semantic processing of kanji. Ph.D. diss., Northeastern University.

186   Selected References

Best, C., ed. 1985. *Hemispheric Function and Collaboration in the Child.* New York: Academic Press.

Bogen, J. E. 1985. The callosal syndrome. In *Clinical Neuropsychology,* ed. K. M. Heilman and E. Valenstein, 295–338. New York: Oxford University Press.

———. 1986. One brain, two brains, or both? In *Two Hemispheres, One Brain: Functions of the Corpus Callosum,* ed. F. Leporé, M. Ptito, and H. H. Jasper. New York: Allan R. Liss.

———. 1969. The other side of the brain, 1–3. *Bull. LA Neur. Soc.* 34, no. 3.

———. 1977. Some educational aspects of hemispheric specialization. *UCLA Ed.* 17: 24–32.

Bradshaw, J. L., and N. C. Nettleton. 1983. *Human Cerebral Asymmetry.* Englewood, N. J.: Prentice-Hall.

Bryden, M. P. 1990. Choosing sides: The left and right of the normal brain. *Canadian Psych.* 31, no. 4.

———. 1982. *Laterality and Functional Asymmetry in the Intact Brain.* Toronto: Academic Press.

Burns, A. 1989. *The Power of the Written Word: The Role of Literacy in the History of Western Civilization.* New York: Viking.

Butler, C. R., and A. C. Francis. 1973. Split-brain behavior without splitting: Tactile discriminations in monkeys. *Isr. J. Med. Sc.* 9 (Suppl): 79–84.

Caine, G., and R. N. Caine. 1989. Learning about accelerated learning. *Training and Dev. J.* 43: 65–73.

———. 1991. *Making Connections: Teaching and the Human Brain.* Alexandria, VA: Association for Supervision and Curriculum Development.

———. 1990. Understanding a brain-based approach to learning and teaching. *Ed. Leadership* 48: 66–70.

Calvin, W. H. 1994. *Conversations with Neil's Brain: The Neural Nature of Thought and Language.* Reading, Mass.: Addison-Wesley.

Capasso, P. D. 1981. Right brain approach to art: An examination of a drawing process used in a sixth grade classroom. Master's thesis, Pacific University.

Carmon, A., H. W. Gordon, E. Bental, and B. Z. Harnes. 1977. Retraining in literal alexi: Substitution of a right hemisphere perceptual strategy for impaired left hemisphere processing. *Bull. LA Neur. Soc.* 42: 41–50.

Chiarello, C. 1991. Interpretation of word meanings by the cerebral hemispheres: One is not enough. In *The Psychology of Word Meanings,* ed. P. J. Schwanenflugel, 251–78. Hillsdale, N.J.: Lawrence Erlbaum Assoc.

Clark, M. J. 1981. The rejection of psychological approaches to mental disorder in late nineteenth-century British psychiatry. In *Madhouses, Mad-Doctors, and Madmen: The Social History of Psychiatry in the Victorian Era,* ed. A. Scull, 284. Philadelphia: University of Pennsylvania Press.

Corballis, M. C. 1983. *Human Laterality.* New York: Academic Press.

Coren, S. 1992. *The Lefthander Syndrome.* New York: Free Press.

Cowan, W. M., J. W. Fawcett, D. D. M. O'Leary, and B. B. Stanfield. 1984. Regressive events in neurogenesis. *Science* 225: 1258–65.

Cutting, J. 1990. *The Right Cerebral Hemisphere and Psychiatric Disorders.* New York: Oxford University Press.

De Lacoste-Utamsing, C., and R. L. Holloway. 1982. Sexual dimorphism in the human corpus callosum. *Science* 216: 1431–32.

Dimond, S. 1972. *The Double Brain.* London: Churchill Livingstone.

Doty, R. W., W. H. Overman, Jr., and N. Negrão. 1979. Role of forebrain commissures in hemispheric specialization and memory in macaques. In *Structure and Function of Cerebral Commissures,* ed. I. S. Russell, M. W. Van Hof, and G. Berlucchi. Baltimore: University Park Press.

Durden-Smith, J. 1990. Male and female—why? *Quest,* 15–19 October, 93–99.

Edwards, B. 1979. *Drawing on the Right Side of the Brain.* Los Angeles: Tarcher.

Ellenberger, H. F. 1970. *The Discovery of the Unconscious: The History and Evolution of Dynamic Psychiatry.* New York: Basic Books.

Epstein, H., and C. F. Toepfer, Jr. 1978. A neuroscience basis for reorganizing middle grades education. *Ed. Lead.* 35, no. 8: 656–58, 660.

Fernstrom, J., and R. J. Wurtman. 1974. Nutrition and the brain. *Sci. Am.* 230, no. 2: 84–91.

Finger, S. 1994. *Origins of Neuroscience: A History of Explorations into Brain Function.* New York: Oxford University Press.

Fink, K. J. 1991. *Goethe's History of Science.* New York: Cambridge University Press.

Gazzaniga, M. S. 1985. *The Social Brain: Discovering the Networks of the Mind.* New York: Basic Books.

————, J. E. Bogen, and R. W. Sperry. 1962. Some functional effects of sectioning the cerebral commissures in man. *Proc. Natl. Acad. Sci. USA* 48: 1765–69.

————, and J. E. LeDoux. 1978. *The Integrated Mind.* New York: Plenum Press.

Geschwind, N. 1972. Disorders of higher cortical function in children. *Clin. Proc. Ch. Hosp.* 28: 261–72.

————, and P. Behan. 1982. Left-handedness: Association with immune disease, migraine, and developmental learning disorder. *Proc. Natl. Acad. Sci. USA* 79: 5097–5100.

————, and E. Kaplan. 1962. A human cerebral deconnection syndrome. *Neur.* 12: 675–85.

Goodwin, B. 1989. Evolution and the generative order. In *Theoretical Biology: Epigenetic and Evolutionary Order from Complex Systems,* ed. B. Goodwin and P. Saunders, 89–100. Edinburgh: Edinburgh University Press.

————. 1989–90. The evolution of generic forms. In *Organizational Constraints on the Dynamics of Evolution,* ed. G. Vida and J. M. Smith.

————. 1995. *How the Leopard Changed Its Spots: The Evolution of Complexity.* London: Phoenix.

————. 1988. Morphogenesis and heredity. In *Evolutionary Processes and Metaphors,* ed. M.-W. Ho and S. W. Fox, 145–62. New York: John Wiley.

Grady, M. P., and E. A. Luecke. 1978. *Education and the Brain.* Bloomington, Ind.: Phi Delta Kappa Educational Foundation.

Gray, J. A., J. Feldon, J. N. P. Rawlins, et al. 1991. The neuropsychology of schizophrenia. *Beh. and Brain Sci.* 14: 1–84, p. 18.

Green, E. E., A. M. Green, and E. D. Walters. 1970. Voluntary control of internal states: Psychological and physiological. *J. Transp. Psy.* 2: 1–26.

Gregory, J. C. 1931. *A Short History of Atomism.* London: Macmillan.

Harris, L. J. 1975. Functional specialization of the cerebral hemispheres in infants and children: New experimental and clinical evidence. Paper presented at the Biennial Meeting of the Society for Research in Child Development, Denver.

——. 1988. Right brain training: Some reflections on the application of research on cerebral hemispheric specialization to education. In *Brain Lateralization in Children: Developmental Implications,* ed. D. L. Molfese and S. J. Segalowitz, 207–35. New York.

——. 1980. Which hand is the "eye" of the blind? A new look at an old question. In *The Neuropsychology of Left Handedness,* ed. J. Herron. New York: Academic Press.

Harris, W. V. 1989. *Ancient Literacy.* Cambridge: Harvard University Press.

Havelock, E. A. 1982. *The Literate Revolution in Greece.* Princeton: Princeton University Press.

——. 1986. *The Muse Learns to Write.* New Haven: Yale University Press.

——. 1978. Poetic sources of the Greek alphabet. In *Communication Arts in the Ancient World,* ed. Havelock and Hershbell, 21–36. New York: Basic Books.

Heilman, K. M., and E. Valenstein. 1985. *Clinical Neuropsychology.* 2d ed. New York: Oxford University Press.

Hellige, J. B. 1993. *Hemispheric Asymmetry: What's Right and What's Left.* Cambridge: Harvard University Press.

Hicks, R. E., J. M. Frank, and M. Kinsbourne. 1982. The locus of bimanual skill transfer. *J. Gen. Psy.* 107: 277–81.

Hier, D. B. 1979. Sex differences in hemispheric specialization: Hypothesis for the excess of dyslexia in boys. *Bull. Orton Soc.* 29: 74–83.

Holloway, R. L. 1980. Within-species brain-body weight variability: A reexamination of the Danish data and other primate species. *Am. J. Phys. Anth.* 53: 109–21.

Iaccino, J. F. 1993. *Left Brain–Right Brain Differences: Inquiries, Evidences, and New Approaches.* Hillsdale: Erlbaum.

Innocenti, G. M. 1985. Personal communication.

Joanette, Y. 1990. *Right Hemisphere and Verbal Communication.* New York: Singular Books.

Jung, R. 1981. Perception and action. In *Regulatory Functions of the CNS: Principles of Motion and Organization,* ed. J. Szentagothai, M. Palkovitz, and J. Hamori. Oxford: Pergamon Press.

Kandanoff, L. P. 1983. Roads to chaos. *Physics Today,* December, 46–53.

Kimura, D. 1973. The asymmetry of the human brain. *Recent Progress in Perception,* March, 246–54.

Kinsbourne, M. 1986. Relationships between nonright-handedness and diseases of the immune systems. Paper presented at 14th Annual Meeting of the International Neuropsychological Society, Denver.

Kline, C. L., and Kline, C. L. 1975. Follow-up study of 216 dyslexic children. *Bull. Orton Soc.* 25: 127–44.

Koppel, H., and G. M. Innocenti. 1983. Is there a genuine exuberancy of callosal projections in development? A quantitative electron microscopic study in the cat. *Neurosc. Lett.* 41: 33–40.

Kraft, R. H. 1976. An EEG study: Hemispheric brain functioning of six to eight year-old children during Piagetian and curriculum tasks with variation in presentation mode. Ph.D. diss., Ohio State University.

Landis, T., G. Assal, and E. Perret. 1979. Opposite cerebral hemisphere superiorities for visual associative processing of emotional facial expressions and objects. *Nature* 278: 739–40.

Landis, T., R. Graves, and H. Goodglass. 1981. Dissociated awareness of manual performance on two different visual associative tasks: A "split-brain" phenomenon in normal subjects? *Cortex* 17: 435–40.

Levy, J. 1985. Interhemispheric collaboration: Single-mindedness in the asymmetric brain. In *Hemispheric Function and Collaboration in the Child,* ed. C. Best. New York: Academic Press.

Levy, J., and M. Reid. 1978. Variations in cerebral organization as a function of handedness, hand posture in writing, and sex. *J. Exp. Psy. Gen.* 107: 119–44.

Long, D. J. 1977. Is your right brain working? Indiana Dept of Education.

Marks, C. E. 1981. *Commissurotomy, Consciousness, and Unity of Mind.* Cambridge: MIT Press.

Marx, K. 1994. *Right Brain–Left Brain Photography: The Art and Technique of 70 Modern Masters.* New York: Amphoto.

McCarthy, B. 1980. *The 4MAT System: Teaching to Learning Styles with Right–Left Mode Techniques.* Arlington Heights, Ill.: Excel.

Meeker, M. 1981. *SOI Learning Abilities Test.* El Segundo, Calif.: SOI Institute.

Moscovitch, M. 1983. Stages of processing and hemispheric differences in language in the normal subject. In *Psychobiology of Language,* ed. M. Studdert-Kennedy. Cambridge: MIT Press.

Nebes, R. D., and R. W. Sperry. Hemispheric deconnection syndrome with cerebral birth injury in the dominant arm area. *Neuropsy.* 9: 247–59.

Newcomer, C. 1991. *Visions and Dreams.* Windchime Records. Audiocassette.

Noller, R. B., and S. J. Parnes. 1972. The creative studies project. 1: The development. *J. Cr. Beh.* 6, no. 1: 11–22.

O'Dell, D. K. 1981. *Relaxation and Recreation (R & R) for Children.* Unpublished manuscript.

O'Leary, D. S., N. C. Andreasen, R. R. Hurtig, M. L. Kesler, M. Rogers, S. Arndt, T. Cizadlo, G. L. Watkins, L. L. Boles Ponto, P. T. Kirchner, and R. D. Hichwa. 1995. Auditory attentional deficits in patients with schizophrenia: A positron emission tomography study. *Ar. Gen. Psy.* 53: 633–41.

Orton, S. T. 1937. *Reading, Writing, and Speech Problems in Children.* New York: Norton.

Paivio, A. 1971. *Imagery and Verbal Processes.* New York: Raven Press.

Peters, M. 1983a. Differentiation and lateral specialization in motor development. In *Manual Specialization and the Developing Brain,* ed. G. Young, S. J. Segalowitz, C. M. Corter, and S. E. Trehub. New York: Academic Press.

———. 1983b. Inverted and noninverted left handers compared on the basis of motor performance and measures related to the act of writing. *Aust. J. Psy.* 35: 405–16.

Prince, G. M. 1976. The mindspring theory: A new development from synectics research. *J. Cre. Beh.* 9: 159–87.

Proper, D. 1994. Use the Force: The intuitiveness of the right side of the brain can be real handy come bird season. *Field and Stream* 98, no. 10.

Rakic, P., and K. P. Riley. 1983. Overproduction and elimination of retinal axons in the fetal Rhesus monkey. *Science* 219: 1441–44.

Rennels, M. R. 1976. Cerebral symmetry: An urgent concern for education. *Phi Delta Kappan* 57, no. 7: 471–72.

Restak, R. M. 1979. The other difference between boys and girls. *Ed. Lead.* 37, no. 3: 232–35.

Rhawn, J. 1992. *The Right Brain and the Unconscious: Discovering the Stranger Within.* New York: Plenum Press.

Russell, G. A., and I. S. Russell. 1979. Introduction to the beginnings of commissure research. In *Structure and Function of Cerebral Commissures,* ed. I. S. Russell, M. W. Van Hof, and G. Berlucchi. Baltimore: University Park Press.

Salerno, D. P. 1993. Be creative in every class. *Rel. Teach. J.* 27, no. 5.

Sass, L. A. 1992. *Madness and Modernism: Insanity in the Light of Modern Art, Literature, and Thought.* Cambridge: Harvard University Press.

Schott, G. D. 1980. Mirror movements of the left arm following peripheral damage to the preferred right arm. *J. Neurol. Neurosurg. Psy.* 43: 768–73.

Seemes, J., S. Weinstein, L. Ghent, and H. L. Teuber. 1960. *Somatosensory Changes after Penetrating Brain Wounds in Man.* Cambridge: Harvard University Press.

Seidman, L. J. 1983. Schizophrenia and brain dysfunction: An integration of recent neurodiagnostic findings. *Psy. Bull.* 94: 195, 223.

Showalter, E. 1991. *Sexual Anarchy: Gender and Culture at the* Fin de Siècle. New York: Penguin.

Sidtis, J. J., B. T. Volpe, J. E. Holtzman, D. H. Wilson, and M. S. Gazzaniga. 1981. Cognitive interaction after staged callosal section: Evidence for transfer of semantic activation. *Science* 212: 344–46.

Simonov, P. V. 1974. On the role of the hippocampus in the integrative activity of the brain. *Act. Neur. Exp.* 34: 37–38.

Sperry, R. W. 1966. Brain bisection and consciousness. In *Brain and Conscious Experience,* ed. J. C. Eccles. New York: Springer-Verlag.

———. 1974. Lateral specialization in the surgically separated hemispheres. In *The Neurosciences Third Study Program,* ed. F. O. Schmitt and F. G. Worden. Cambridge: MIT Press.

———, and E. Clark. 1949. Interocular transfer of visual discrimination habits in a teleost fish. *Phys. Zool.* 22: 372–78.

Stanish, B. 1989. *The Ambidextrous Mind Book: Creative and Inventive Adventures for the Curriculum.* Carthage, Ill.: Good Apple.

———, and C. Singletary. 1987. *Inventioneering: Nurturing Intellectual Talent in the Classroom.* Carthage, Ill.: Good Apple.

Stewart, I. 1989. *Does God Play Dice? The Mathematics of Chaos.* Oxford: Basil Blackwell.

Tannenbaum, A. J. 1977. Meta learning. Paper presented at Nature and Needs of the Gifted, Columbia University.

Torrance, E. P. 1968. A longitudinal examination of the fourth-grade slump in creativity. *Gift. Ch. Q.* 12, no. 4: 195–99.

Van Hof, M. W. 1979. Interocular transfer and interhemispheric communication in the rabbit. In *Structure and Function of Cerebral Commissures,* ed. I. S. Russell, M. W. Hof, and G. Berlucchi. Baltimore: University Park Press.

Walkup, L. E. 1965. Creativity in science through visualization. *Per. Mot. Sk.* 21: 35–41.

Wells, C. G. 1991. *Right Brain Sex.* New York: Prentice-Hall.

Weylman, S. T., H. H. Brownell, and H. Gardner. 1988. It's what you mean, not what you say: Pragmatic language use in brain-damaged patients. In *Language, Communication, and the Brain,* ed. F. Plum, 229–43. New York: Raven.

Wheatley, G. H. 1977. The right hemisphere's role in problem solving. *Ar. Tea.* 25: 36–39.

Wigan, A. L. 1844. *The Duality of the Mind. Proved by the Structure, Functions, and Diseases of the Brain, and by the Phenomena of Mental Derangement, and Shewn to Be Essential to Moral Responsibility.* London: Longman, Brown, Green, and Longmans.

Williams, L. V. 1983. *Teaching for the Two-Sided Mind: A Guide to Right Brain–Left Brain Education.* New Jersey: Spectrum.

Wilson, C. 1991. *Frankenstein's Castle: The Right Brain, Door to Wisdom.* Bath: Avon.

Witelson, S. F. 1983. Bumps on the brain: Right-left anatomic asymmetry as a key to functional asymmetry. In *Language Functions and Brain Organization,* ed. S. Segalowitz. New York: Academic Press.

———. 1985. On hemisphere specialization and cerebral plasticity from birth. Mark 2. In *Hemispheric Function and Collaboration in the Child,* ed. C. Best. New York: Academic Press.

Wurtman, R. 1982. Nutrients that modify brain function. *Sci. Am.* 246, no. 4: 50–59.

Yakovlev, P. I., and A. Lecours. 1967. The myelogenetic cycles of re-
    gional maturation of the brain. In *Regional Development of the
    Brain in Early Life,* ed. A. Minkowski. London: Blackwell.
Zaidel, D., and R. W. Sperry. 1974. Memory impairment after commis-
    surotomy in man. *Brain* 97: 263–72.
———. 1973 Performance on the raven's colored progressive ma-
    trices by subjects with cerebral commissurotomy. *Cortex* 9: 33–39.
Zaidel, E. 1983. Disconnection syndrome as a model for laterality ef-
    fects in the normal brain. In *Cerebral Hemisphere Asymmetry: Method,
    Theory, and Application,* ed. J. B. Hellige. New York: Praeger.
Zipursky, R. B., et al. 1991. Brain size in schizophrenia. *Ar. Gen. Psy.*
    48: 179–81.

Index